MW00532783

Praise for

MAKING YOUR MARRIAGE A FORTRESS

Marital storms are a reality in human experience. They come with different levels of intensity, and in different seasons of life, but none of us are exempt. If you are looking for practical help in surviving the storms, *Making Your Marriage a Fortress* is a must-read.

GARY CHAPMAN, PhD, author of *The 5 Love Languages*

There are so many challenges today that can impact our marriages. When real issues arise, we need more than pep talks and Band-Aids; we need wise guidance and practical tools! Well, Gary Thomas is a wise guide who provides great tools. He is also one of the most caring men I know. This book is an opportunity to learn from an insightful pastor who has a lot of experience and who cares about you and your marriage. It will help you come out stronger on the other side.

SHAUNTI FELDHAHN, social researcher and bestselling author of *For Women Only*, *For Men Only*, and *Surprising Secrets of Highly Happy Marriages*

Gary Thomas's *Sacred Marriage* provides the transcendent foundation of biblical marriage, while *Making Your Marriage a Fortress* gives us a look inside at the practical application of when God's Word intersects with the problems of living we all experience in a fallen world.

STEPHEN D. WILKE, PhD, founder, LEADon University

With real-life stories, Gary Thomas's always-authentic style and shared knowledge from some of the best marriage advocates today make this a masterpiece of wisdom. From dating and engagement times to the most seasoned marriage, this book offers guidance through every season and storm. The takeaways at the end of each chapter are gold.

BOB RAUSCHER, pastor and marriage coach
(www.themarriagepastor.com)

Now, more than ever, our marriages are under siege. Now, more than ever, we need them to be fortresses. Gary Thomas's sage wisdom— pulling in stories from all across the body of Christ and weaving them with God's Word—is fortress building. At twenty-plus years into marriage, I have found this book to be a gift to read.

SARA HAGERTY, bestselling author of *Unseen* and *ADORE*

Every good marriage bumps into bad things. It's inevitable. But if you guard your relationship with intention, if you cultivate emotional safety, you can make it through nearly any difficulty to say, "I love you more than I did before." The key, of course, is to prepare for tough times—to make your marriage a fortress. That's why Gary Thomas's outstanding book is invaluable for every couple who is serious about enjoying life-long love to the fullest.

DRS. LES AND LESLIE PARROTT, authors of *Saving Your Marriage Before It Starts* and *I Love You More*

MAKING
YOUR
MARRIAGE
A FORTRESS

MAKING YOUR MARRIAGE A FORTRESS

Strengthening Your
MARRIAGE to Withstand
LIFE'S STORMS

Gary Thomas

Bestselling Author of *Sacred Marriage*

ZONDERVAN
BOOKS

ZONDERVAN BOOKS

Making Your Marriage a Fortress
Copyright © 2022 by The Center for Evangelical Spirituality

Requests for information should be addressed to:
Zondervan, 3900 Sparks Dr. SE, Grand Rapids, Michigan 49546

Zondervan titles may be purchased in bulk for educational, business, fundraising, or sales promotional use. For information, please email SpecialMarkets@Zondervan.com.

ISBN 978-0-310-34748-4 (international trade paper edition)
ISBN 978-0-310-36610-2 (audio)

Library of Congress Cataloging-in-Publication Data
Names: Thomas, Gary (Gary Lee), author.
Title: Making your marriage a fortress : strengthening your marriage to withstand life's storms / Gary Thomas.
Description: Grand Rapids : Zondervan, 2022. | Summary: "Written by the bestselling author of Sacred Marriage, Gary Thomas, Making Your Marriage a Fortress imparts the wisdom and insight couples need to fortify their marriage before trials come, keep their marriage together when they come, and enjoy a marriage that is stronger after they come"—Provided by publisher.
Identifiers: LCCN 2022010482 (print) | LCCN 2022010483 (ebook) | ISBN 9780310347453 (hardcover) | ISBN 9780310347460 (ebook)
Subjects: LCSH: Marriage—Religious aspects—Christianity. | Marital quality. | BISAC: RELIGION / Christian Living / Love & Marriage | RELIGION / Christian Living / Spiritual Growth
Classification: LCC BV835 .T46935 2022 (print) | LCC BV835 (ebook) | DDC 248.8/44—dc23/eng /20220705
LC record available at https://lccn.loc.gov/2022010482
LC ebook record available at https://lccn.loc.gov/2022010483

Published in association with Yates & Yates, www.yates2.com.

Cover design: Micah Kandros
Cover illustration: Alex Gontar / Shutterstock
Interior design: Sara Colley

Printed in the United States of America

22 23 24 25 26 27 28 29 30   /LSC/   12 11 10 9 8 7 6 5 4 3 2 1

To Mary Kay Smith and her husband, Brad.
Post Sacred Pathways, *Mary Kay has read and reviewed*
every one of my books prior to its publication.
She and Brad have become friends
and true coworkers in the advance of God's kingdom.
I'm grateful for her friendship, competence, advice,
perspective, and partnership in this ministry.

CONTENTS

INTRODUCTION

The Big One

Lisa and I were enjoying a weekend in Fredericksburg, Texas, a quaint, tourist-oriented town nestled in the Lone Star State's Hill Country.

That's when the phone call came.

"Gary, this is going to be a big one."

Ben isn't one to panic. He's a low-drama kind of guy. But he urged Lisa and me to get back to Houston right away. The fact that he made the phone call was sobering enough. His words, given the source, sounded even more ominous. Essentially, he was telling me, "I know you've laughed at the way we've panicked about storms in the past, but this isn't panic. This is real."

Ben was referring to the fact that, coming from the Pacific Northwest, I had occasionally remarked about the way Texans could cancel school for a week if it looked like we might get a quarter inch of snow. We'd heard rumor after rumor of big storms in Texas and seen the flashing digital road signs appear every June: "It's Hurricane Season! Prepare for an Emergency!" For the first few years we read the signs and took them seriously. Now, in year seven of our Texas residency, we thought those warnings were about as relevant as the permanent "This Bridge Will Be Icy in Freezing Weather" signs that came into play in Houston approximately once every five years.

To be honest, most of the storm warnings *had* turned out to be puddles in comparison to storms we had seen in the Northwest. But when Ben, of all people, told me something was different about Harvey, Lisa and I figured we should cut short our time away and get back to our house in Houston.

Hours after we arrived, Harvey hit the coast hard but then immediately weakened.

That's not so bad, I thought. Devastating for Rockport, yes, but everything was still standing in downtown Houston.

That's when Harvey decided to camp out for a while and proceeded to dump more than fifty inches of rain over the next three days.

LANDFALL

At the time, we lived in an area of Houston called "the Heights." Lisa and I laughed when we learned that the name "Heights" arose from the fact that our neighborhood is a couple dozen feet higher than downtown Houston. Apparently, a couple dozen feet of altitude in flat Houston demanded a geographical moniker, and since we moved here after spending most of our lives in sight of the Cascade Range, we felt right at home.

In the aftermath of Harvey, we stopped laughing about that couple dozen feet. Two dozen feet isn't much, but when you're dealing with rising water, you'll take every inch the land gives you.

Once the rains started, they didn't stop. They were forceful, pelting, thunderous at times, and unrelenting. The drainage ditches filled first, then our sidewalks were covered, then the water rose about halfway up our vehicles' wheels. We started searching on the internet for how to waterproof our house, but it was much too late for that, as we didn't have any of the necessary tools or supplies. My pathetic stash of painter's tape and cardboard was no match for rising water.

By the time Harvey rolled back out into the Gulf of Mexico, more than one hundred people were dead and more than a hundred billion dollars of damage had been done.

Though our house stayed dry, thousands of people in our community lost their homes. Some had to move upstairs when their downstairs became an indoor pool. In one heartbreaking story, some friends of ours had stayed dry through the worst of the rains, but near the end of the storm, authorities opened up a dam they feared might be breached, and the ensuing water surge sent six inches of water into their house for six hours.

Six inches isn't much and six hours isn't long, but when you're talking about water in a house, it was enough to do catastrophic damage.

One of the guys in my running group lived in a neighborhood that became a lake. We were told of a wealthy medical professional who paid more than six thousand dollars to essentially shrink-wrap his house in anticipation of the storm, but it didn't work. His house still became a sponge.

Finally, Lisa and I got it. Yes, there had been years of near misses and what ended up being pointless panic. But Harvey was so bad for so long that we would never again look down on anyone taking storm warnings seriously.

Hurricanes are an inevitable part of living so close to the Gulf. If you stay in Houston for years rather than just months, you'll eventually have your own storm story to share. There are many benefits of living in this part of the Lone Star State, but with the good come the hurricanes. It's just a matter of time.

The same principle is true for your marriage. Your storm is just around the corner. I can't tell you where it will hit, when it will hit, or how it will hit. I just know that you live in a world where spiritual, physical, relational, financial, emotional, and health-related storms are inevitable. Eventually, one will find its way to your house. Your house may be standing tall and proud in pleasant weather, but can it survive a storm?

YOUR HURRICANE IS COMING

I'm embarrassingly sentimental when I perform the marriage ceremony for a couple. Lisa and I spend so long counseling each couple that we grow to love them dearly, and I'm seriously awed by the weighty commitment these young people (and occasionally middle-aged people) are making. I try so hard to prepare them, but I can't fully prepare them because the reality is, none of us know when we get married just how difficult the journey may be—not just because of the fact of our sin (which is the focus of *Sacred Marriage*), not just because relationships tend to drift (which is the focus of *A Lifelong Love*), and not just because familiarity tends to breed contempt (which is the focus of *Cherish*), but because we live in a broken and sometimes even hostile world that assaults all relationships. Life will occasionally be brutal, often prove unyielding, and sometimes seem relentlessly unfair.

In this book, we'll look at a couple whose lives have been upended by multiple sclerosis. Another couple who lost their only child. A couple who, because of the husband's vocation, have spent years apart. A wife who had an affair, a couple who earned and lost millions of dollars, and a couple whose home was overturned by an international pandemic no one saw coming. And yet—this is the key point—each couple is now stronger than they were before the crisis hit. They are closer, more mature, more loving, and more committed to their marriage. Somehow the assault ended up pushing them together, even though at the onset it may have felt like their relationship was doomed.

Why weren't their marriages doomed? What caused their relationship to take the hit, stagger, catch its breath, and then come back stronger than ever?

That's what this book is all about.

You may never face their specific challenges (and I earnestly hope you don't), but you'll surely face your own. Financial calamity, health crises, children rebelling or dying or needing lifelong care, personal addictions, busy schedules, forced time apart—the relational hurricanes that married couples face today are legion. Money can't solve these problems. I'll never forget talking with a man whose net worth totaled several billion dollars. Two of his children face a challenge that the best doctors in the world can't solve. He would gladly pay hundreds of millions to make the problem go away, but dollars are powerless and irrelevant against the challenges his children face.

Neither does faith always remove the challenges. Like money, faith can help us deal with the pain and difficulties such challenges present, but also like money, faith doesn't always make them go away.

Romantic love doesn't solve problems either. Romantic love is about as effective in overcoming life's disappointments as trying to hold water in a paper bag. There's not much romance to be enjoyed when a relentless cancer saps a loved one's strength or when you're humiliated because you're being forced to sell your house and your adult children look at you with contempt as they offer you financial advice.

This book is about how to keep your marriage together when the world is determined to rip the two of you apart and, as of right now, how to start making your marriage a fortress in *anticipation* of that unknown assault. When I thought about preparing our home to face Harvey after the storm had hit, it was much too late. If our home had been built with bricks going up twenty feet, we wouldn't have given one of the century's largest storms a moment's thought.

When hurricanes hit, one of two things will be true for you relationally—(1) the state of your marriage will become part of the problem, adding to your woes, or (2) the strength of your marriage will become a refuge against the storm. The couples you're about to meet will admit that they made many mistakes along the way, and they will freely share what they got wrong and where they had to backtrack and find healing. But they'll also share the things they've learned to prepare themselves for the next storm. I was profoundly inspired talking to them; this project has been one of the highlights of my life as I gleaned wisdom and inspiration from wise, godly, and faith-filled sisters and brothers in the Lord.

Here's what I've found: *Getting through one storm is no guarantee that you're set for life* and get to go into retirement. On the contrary, storms often come in threes—a parenting crisis coupled with a health crisis lead to a financial crisis. Or it may be a sin crisis exacerbated by a betrayal crisis made even worse by a vocational crisis. This world is creative in its fallenness and gifted in its ability to undermine even the best of our intentions.

If your house has been "flooded," these stories, and the principles that follow, will assure you that someone else has been where you are and has become immeasurably stronger individually and more intimate as a couple. If you're like Lisa and me, the first six years we lived in Texas, downplaying the warnings because we thought they would never amount to much, I hope you'll take these stories as preparatory planning. Just because you can't see the storm doesn't mean it isn't forming somewhere far off in the ocean, amassing its fury to mock your sense of security.

Most chapters will focus primarily on one couple's story, but the principles gleaned from their struggle will be universal. It's not really about the problems; it's about the principles. If you are strong physically, you can lift up a fallen comrade in battle, open up a jar for your spouse, or help your friend move some heavy furniture. Strength that comes from one source still has many applications; the same is true for spiritual strength: "Godliness has value for all things" (1 Timothy 4:8).

If there's one thing Lisa and I learned from being caught in a hurricane with nothing but painter's tape and cardboard to save our house from an unrelenting flood, it's this: If we wait until the storm hits to gather what we need (i.e., learn these lessons), we've waited too long. Preparation is key to make sure our marriage becomes part of the solution instead of part of the problem.

Though I've never met you, I love you in the Lord, and I want to serve your marriage. I want your relationship to thrive, to be a refuge in the midst of life's storms and inspire many others as you become "more than conquerors" through him who loves you

(Romans 8:37). Please read this book as a labor of love inspired by a God who knows the future you don't know, who has given you witnesses to his steadfast love when you can't see it for yourself, and who can prepare you to draw ever closer to Christ and ever closer to each other.

CHAPTER 1

· · · · · · · · · · · · · · ·

FIGHTING FEAR WITH FAITH

Mentally Managing Loss

What if your biggest fear about your marriage came true? What if you woke up one day and realized that the primary reason you got married is something that now will never happen and has forever been taken away from you?

Can your marriage survive that?

Yes, it can, with faith.

For Stacy and Darell, a sobering diagnosis of multiple sclerosis (MS) reset all their expectations about what their marriage would be like. For you, the diagnosis may be something entirely different—childlessness, a mental illness, the lack of sexual function, or financial impoverishment. Learning to live without what you once thought was a primary purpose of marriage is necessary to find happiness in marriage, for the simple reason that none of us will ever get all we want out of marriage, or at least not for our entire lives.

To succeed in marriage, then, we must succeed in mentally

managing loss. If we don't learn to turn disappointment into determination, helplessness into hope, and frustration into faith, our marriage won't go far in a hostile world.

We all have different fears, but MS hit both Darell and Stacy in core places of their identity, and yet not only has their marriage survived; it has also thrived precisely because of what they learned from having to face down their greatest fears.

TRUE STRENGTH

Stacy fell in love with a weight lifter who could bench-press four hundred pounds. If you're not familiar with weight lifting, that's a lot (and likely a couple hundred pounds more than your spouse could bench press). Stacy's family of origin was neither safe nor healthy. Looking back, she thinks Darell's strength made her feel protected and secure.

It wasn't primarily Darell's physical strength that attracted Stacy, however. "The fact is, before Darell I was drawn more to the small and lean type, the long-distance runners. But when I saw Darell's heart for people—especially youth—experienced the way he truly listened to me, and saw his deep faith, I was hooked. And it didn't hurt that he was wicked funny."

For his part, being physically strong was a core element of Darell's identity. He was never into shaping his physique like bodybuilders do; he just wanted to be a guy who could take care of and protect his wife and family. And he could tell that Stacy wasn't exactly turned off by his arms and pecs. "I was arrogant enough to think that I kind of had a little bit of that 'wow factor.'"

They were married in 1986. Stacy had her strong, protective man who could lift anything, carry in all the groceries, and even pick her up if needed.

Less than three years later, Darell experienced his first early sign of MS—optic neuritis, an inflammation of the optic nerve. It came and went rather quickly, so neither of them paid much attention to it until it returned in 1991, which led doctors to make an official MS diagnosis.

Stacy was pregnant with their second child when they found out.

Even after the diagnosis, Darell's MS lay fairly dormant for a number of years, to the point that Stacy thought perhaps God had healed her husband.

Darell didn't share his wife's belief. "I didn't feel healed. I thought the MS was just hiding under a rock. I didn't share all this with Stacy, but I knew something was up because I kept getting so tired and I could tell my legs weren't working like they used to after a long day of work."

One year in particular brought numerous stressful challenges that overloaded Darell's system. An accident at the camp where he worked, myriad vocational stresses, and some personal challenges all combined to send his body into a tailspin. Darell noticed a major shift in his body's movement as he tried to run to the scene of the accident.

"I couldn't pick up my foot and thought, *Okay, that's not a good thing.*"

Stress can exacerbate the symptoms of MS, and Darell believes that year sent him over the edge. "I've never been the same physically."

INITIAL IMPACT

When you realize life has changed, and that what you hoped to get out of marriage will not come true, it can take a while to accept it.

How do you and your spouse face your fears? Typically, one spouse will deny them while the other obsesses over them—the typical "glass half full, glass half empty" dichotomy. Sometimes couples fight about everything *but* what they're afraid of. Fear unaddressed can become anger, defensiveness, resentment, shame, and any number of secondary emotions. That's why it can help so much to pull up the roots and face your fears by naming them as *fears*.

"I can't bear the thought we'll never have biological children."

"So you're blaming me because I'm infertile?"

That sounds so cruel, so the "fertile" spouse may just shut up and never say what they are truly afraid of. They aren't blaming the other, but they are devastated by the new reality. Facing these issues takes a high degree of differentiation. You must be willing to understand and bear your spouse's frustrations and disappointments without making it about you—even though, of course, it feels like it has everything to do with you. But you didn't choose to be infertile, any more than Darell chose to have MS.

The reason I say we need to deal with fears openly is that fear unaddressed becomes a relational cancer.

Stacy recalls vacationing at an Oregon beach cabin with friends as the recent MS diagnosis hung in the ether between them.

"It was really hard," Stacy remembers.

> We yelled a lot at each other. I yelled a lot at God. Looking back, I think it was all about facing this terrifying reality of the completely unknown. All of a sudden, there's this spike in your

foot, and no doctor can take it out. Your foot is never going to be the same again. It's sort of like how it must have been for Adam and Eve in the Garden after they sinned. Everything was *so* good, but then this event happened. Imagine comparing a sinless marriage, without death and disease, to one with sin, death, and disease! There must have been an ominous feeling that things were never going to be the same. That's what I had to come to grips with.

Face your fears by naming your fears, even if it's initially painful to do so. Naming your fear doesn't make it worse, just as denying it doesn't make it go away. And talking about your fears shouldn't be seen as *blaming* your spouse; it's *helping* your spouse understand you so the two of you can face your disappointments together.

ONE MEDICINE DOESN'T CURE ALL

Darell didn't share Stacy's anger. "For better or for worse, I tend to be the optimist. I always figure things will work out somehow."

Darell doesn't see his way of thinking as better, however. MS forced each of them to draw on spiritual resources they never had before. "I needed a reality check, and Stacy needed some encouragement."

This is such a key principle for facing the moment in marriage when your dreams die. *Each spouse needs a different spiritual prescription. And the one spiritual medicine that heals you may not help your spouse.* Darell needed to face reality; Stacy needed to embrace hope and faith.

A common experience we'll see with most of the couples in this book is that when a spiritual disease assaults a marriage, it hits each spouse in a different way and therefore requires different care. *The symptoms and therefore the cure may look different for each of you.* Respect that. Learn from each other. Understand each other.

Stacy kept saying, "It's going to be horrible" while Darell, true to his nature, kept saying, "It'll all work out." Neither of them had a clue about how wrong and right they both were.

In fact, Darell's optimism initially made things worse. As an athlete, he prided himself in pushing through the pain and working out hard, but for an MS patient that can be counterproductive.

> I tried to stay in shape to prove to myself that I was going to beat MS, until the doctors explained that the more active I was, the more irreparable damage MS was doing to my body.
>
> I finally had to come to the realization that, even as an optimist, it was essential to admit that there was an elephant in the room called MS. I couldn't defeat it. I could manage it, but denying it not only wouldn't get me very far. It would actually take me back quite a bit.

It tore Darell up inside to finally admit that while his body was the host of MS, MS was impacting Stacy's life—indeed their entire family—in a way he couldn't protect them from. His identity had been "I'm the strong man," but he couldn't protect his family from *this*.

So after you name your fear, accept the reality of the new situation. You don't like what it's calling you to do, but there's no use denying it. You need to live and relate to each other accordingly. "This is our new normal. How do we make it work?"

If you're facing down a fear this very moment, pause here and talk about it together. What is your new normal? What do you hate about it? What do you fear about it? In the midst of your own struggle, try to understand how this trial is affecting your spouse, perhaps in a different way than it is affecting you. Use the fear to increase understanding and empathy rather than letting it foster alienation and resentment.

EARNEST ENLIGHTENMENT

Christian transformation looks like this: "Be transformed by the renewing of your mind" (Romans 12:2). To face your own disappointments, you need enlightenment. The Christian classics stress how self-understanding is almost as important as an understanding of God.

John Owen wrote, "He . . . who is not exactly skilled in the knowledge of himself, will never be disentangled from one temptation or another all his days."[1] And Teresa of Ávila wrote, "Knowing ourselves is something so important that I wouldn't want any relaxation ever in this regard."[2] I could cite many other classics, but frankly, common sense alone should carry the argument. Growth depends on seeing things as they are; otherwise, we don't really know what's wrong and therefore aren't aware of what we need to change. Most of us live with a faulty view of ourselves and of God, so we stumble along like a person with a fever who thinks they need medicine for an upset stomach, or a person with a brain tumor who thinks they just need to do Pilates to improve their balance. We need the courage of David to pray, "Search me, God, and know my heart; test me and know my anxious thoughts.

See if there is any offensive way in me, and lead me in the way everlasting" (Psalm 139:23–24).

David models to us the need to *seek* the truth, not just believe the truth, and he assumes he needs God to show him what lies hidden. He learned this the hard way. Remember, David actually thought he was okay, before Nathan courageously challenged him—saying, "You are the man!" (2 Samuel 12:7)—and the full depth of his sin with Uriah and Bathsheba was exposed in all its ugly horror. When was the last time you asked God to search your heart? When was the last time you listened for the Holy Spirit to quicken your conscience?

Now is a good time to begin. Life's disappointments, if faced with the proper attitude, can force us into reevaluating who we are, who our spouse is, what God offers, and what we actually need. And they can awaken us to greater self-awareness. Stacy looks back and says:

> Who knows who they are when they are newly married? Both Darell and I came from really challenging home lives and households, though early on, we didn't realize how much our backgrounds had affected us. The subconscious reality for me was that I married Darell because I wanted someone like that to take care of me. It's ironic, because now I'm taking care of him.

Why did *you* get married? What hopes did you think your spouse would fulfill? Have those hopes been dashed? Can you still find meaning and purpose in your marriage in the face of your disappointments?

One thing many of the classic Christian writers such as Madame Guyon, Teresa of Ávila, Julian of Norwich, and Henry

Drummond (and in contemporary times, Kay Warren) stress is the Christian practice of *surrender*. Many of us don't realize how frequently and earnestly we fight with God. We will not give up! Our expectations will be met! Our hopes will not be dashed! We will make life work the way we want it to!

Until we can't.

Surrender is the humble acknowledgment that life is about conceding to and accepting God's agenda and will over our own, seeking to learn what he wants us to learn instead of trying to convince God that what we initially wanted is best.

Both Stacy and Darell had to embrace surrender in order to move forward. Darell explains: "As a young man, I just wanted to be strong physically. God wanted me to see that inside, there was way more to me than just my physical strength."

Stacy had to accept that the help she was seeking might come from a different source than her husband. "For so many years, I thought my husband would take care of me and be strong and protect me and provide for me, and now the very thing I wanted most, and one of the reasons I sought to get married, God was saying about it, 'No, that's not going to happen. *I'm* going to care for you.'"

She doesn't sentimentalize how excruciating the process of surrender is. "Working out the death of our expectations and receiving God's counteroffer is rarely pretty. Accepting the new reality can be really hard."

Darell had to go through the same process:

> I told Stacy in my wedding vows that I would take care of her and protect her because she grew up not being protected and cared for. That was my heart. Now I'm in a situation where she

takes care of me and protects me, and I'm haunted that I haven't been able to live up to that vow, but those vows were said as a young adult.

When I was first diagnosed, I was riddled with fear. All of my prayers had to do with being healed. I recited every healing passage in the Bible and proclaimed them loudly to God (as if he had forgotten them). It was all, 'Heal me, heal me, heal me.' Finally—we're talking years here—God got through to me with, 'Darell, I get that you want to be healed of MS, but I have something even better for you. Just hang with me. There are bigger problems in your life than MS, and I can use MS to address those things.

When I interview people of faith like Stacy and Darell, I'm often blown away by such massive declarations of faith. No human being on their own comes up with, "There are bigger issues in my life than MS." That's God. He spoke clearly and with comfort in a way Darell could receive it.

"I said, 'Okay, God, let's go, but would you do one thing? Could you take the fear away?' and I believe God said, 'I can do that,' and that moment, *I was healed.* Not of MS! I was healed of my fear, which was a bigger issue than MS."

He knew the healing was complete one night when he realized, "Darell, here you are, in a wheelchair, just what you wanted to never happen, and yet you're not afraid. You're still laughing. Your wife is still with you. You have a good life."

Stacy knew her reset had taken place one evening as she paused during a dinner party to look around. "We had a table full of people laughing and enjoying the evening, and it dawned on me: Darell is in a wheelchair, my greatest fear, *and we're doing it.*

We're managing it. I thought, *What damage those ten years of fear did, and yet here we are.* In the end, those fears did more damage to us than the MS."

Darell adds, "A lot of times we can pray for the wrong thing. A lot of great things have come out of living more than half my life with MS. I'm closer to what God wants me to be."

I would be remiss to pass over the power of Darell's casual "A lot of great things have come out of living over half my life with MS." That's an astonishing statement, but it can be true of any marital challenge. It's a hard-won affirmation of Romans 8:28–29:

> And we know that in all things God works for the good of those who love him, who have been called according to his purpose. For those God foreknew he also predestined to be conformed to the image of his Son.

I recommend great caution before you take out this verse when trying to encourage a hurting friend. Wrongly applied, it can feel like salt poured into a fresh wound. But when people apply it to *themselves* after God smashes their expectations, this declaration helps them crawl through their fears and prepares their hearts to receive the truth of God's affirmation. It just may be one of the most powerful statements in Scripture.

A MARITAL RESET

After you reset your own expectations, you need to reset the expectations you have for your marriage. Stacy remembers:

Before MS, we were like a hand-in-glove couple. I used to *love* riding in Darell's wake. I didn't need to do anything myself because I could follow in his wake. When I realized it wouldn't be that way anymore [Darell is now retired, and Stacy is still working], I responded by trying to control everything, still trying to produce the outcome that desperately hung on in my head: Darell would be the strong, charismatic, up-front guy everyone looked up to, and I'd be his support. I couldn't get that out of my head.

Sadly, in my attempt to make that happen, I became a very controlling and enabling wife and mother. I started doing everything and putting it all on me. If God wasn't going to fix this, I'd do my best to fix as much of it as I could. I tried to create an environment so that in every aspect Darell wouldn't have to do anything. It was a desperate attempt to preserve his strength and health. I kind of stopped becoming me and became the environment controller. That enabled everyone in my family to think, *Oh, Mom will just do it.*

Are you making things worse by your response? In some ways, Stacy believes her attitude hurt her family more than MS did. Maybe your *reaction* to financial scarcity or childlessness is becoming a bigger problem in your marriage than the initial assault.

How do you avoid this? You have to learn how to live without your expectations, and that may be as shaky an experience as a first-time driver attempting to parallel park. There may be some awkward moments and a slightly dented bumper or two. But that's the beauty of lifelong marriage—we usually have time to make our first attempt, get it wrong, re-evaluate, and try again.

It took *decades* for Darell and Stacy to get to where they are today. Maturity is a *process*. It's not about getting everything right the first time. It's often about taking a wrong turn, ending up at a dead end, turning around, and finally asking God for the right directions.

One of the best tools for growth is learning how to grieve in a healthy way. Stacy, the "glass half empty" part of the couple, wants to emphasize that "it's important to be okay to grieve and to be sad. Don't just be *mad*; give yourself space to truly *grieve*. And when you have children, talk with them about grieving. When our daughter got into middle school and her dad showed up at events with a walker, we thought she was embarrassed, which of course was hurtful. Later, we realized she wasn't embarrassed; she was grieving, which is healthy and needful. We kind of put her in that situation because, back then, both Darell and I always put up a front—'We're going to do this; our lives are not going to be any different'—but that's a lie. Our lives were going to be very different, and it's okay to grieve about that."

Grieving isn't sinful. It's healthy to admit to God where you hurt, how you hurt, and what makes you hurt. Mixed with an attitude of surrender, grieving is a necessary step toward spiritual health, maturity, and a life of faith.

D. A. Carson writes, "There is no attempt in Scripture to whitewash the anguish of God's people when they undergo suffering. They argue with God, they complain to God, they weep before God. Theirs is not a faith that leads to dry-eyed stoicism, but a faith so robust it wrestles with God."[3]

As Esther Fleece points out in her excellent book *No More Faking Fine*, God the Father grieves (Genesis 6:5–6), Jesus grieves (John 11:35), and the Holy Spirit grieves (Isaiah 63:10), so grieving cannot in itself be an act of sin.[4] Instead, it's often a courageous and honest step toward a life of faith. Far from pushing God away, lament brings him near: "The LORD is close to the brokenhearted and saves those who are crushed in spirit" (Psalm 34:18).

CELEBRATE

Darell, the "glass half full" part of the couple, is quick to add, "Yes, grieving is very important, but at some point you need to stop grieving and start celebrating what you have."

His perspective here humbles me. "Let's say I have 20 percent of my physical ability left. I want to use 100 percent of that 20 percent to be productive. Make the most of what you have left. I don't think God is expecting you to be as productive as you were before, but if you just have 20 percent, do 100 percent of that 20 percent."

Let's say you and your spouse are unable to have a biological child. Perhaps you can adopt. Or perhaps you can be the best aunt and uncle in the world. Everyone's situation is different. You may never have what you wanted at first, but don't let your previous expectations take away joy from the opportunities in front of you.

In my research for one of my previous books, I talked to a couple whose husband's cancer treatment meant he and his wife aren't able to enjoy penetrative intercourse. But they are learning to embrace what they can enjoy. Anger and bitterness can lead us to say, "If I can't have everything, I'm not going to do anything." That mindset punishes us more than it heals us. Let's do what we can.

In Darell's case, "I try to get in bed by myself, but Stacy has to pull my legs over once I do. But I don't just sit there in the chair and expect her to do everything. I do as much as I can while I can.

And I'm grateful I can at least get in bed myself. I don't take that for granted anymore."

This is where grace becomes sweet. "I'm learning more and more to let my appreciation be greater than my frustration. Every little thing seems to be so hard all the time. The more I take time to appreciate Stacy and everything she does for me, if I can make that greater than my frustration, I find that I appreciate Stacy more and am frustrated less." Do you see how this terrible disease makes Darell love Stacy more rather than less? MS is a terrible thing to endure, yet facing it is making their marriage a fortress far more than it is assaulting their fortress.

"I'd rather be a happy person than a cranky old bitter dude. If I can spend my time appreciating what Stacy does—and she does a lot—instead of fixating on what MS takes away, I should be appreciative all the time. Having MS makes me a more thankful husband than I might have been otherwise."

Having MS makes me a more thankful husband than I might have been otherwise. Astonishing! In the world's eyes, it would be just the opposite, but this is a supernatural truth. Darell focuses on what his wife gives to him, not what MS takes away, and that leads to joy and gratitude instead of resentment.

To get to this place of surrender, we need divine intervention: grace.

LIVING BY GRACE, NOT HEALING

When the apostle Paul asked for his "thorn in the flesh" to be taken away, God responded, "My grace is sufficient for you, for my power is made perfect in weakness," which led Paul to conclude,

"Therefore I will boast all the more gladly about my weaknesses, so that Christ's power may rest on me" (2 Corinthians 12:9).

Darell admits that in his early prayers, "I didn't want grace, I wanted healing." As you face the challenges in your own marriage, are you praying for grace or healing? It's not wrong to pray for healing, but seek grace as you pursue healing. Physical or emotional healing isn't a given, but grace is.

Darell explains, "Paul had to come to grips with the fact that healing wasn't in his story but grace was in his story. And guess what? As he started experiencing grace, he said, 'Grace is better than healing!' Power is made perfect in weakness. And since power was such a big deal to me back then, I had to learn that spiritual grace is better than physical power."

Grace can even cause what might kill a marriage to bring a thrill to marriage. If someone saw Darell and Stacy getting ready for bed or waking up in the morning, they might feel sorry for them—but in doing so, they'd be sadly mistaken. Darell and Stacy are one of the most grateful couples I've ever met.

Stacy explains why: "Thankfulness comes from practice. Darell gets a lot of opportunity to practice because I have to do a lot for him."

Darell adds, "Thankfulness is a choice. I can be frustrated, or I can be thankful."

Stacy has to work at thanksgiving as well:

I have to take on more household duties and caregiving. Doing those chores one time doesn't mean they won't have to be done again tomorrow or the day after that. They will. That's why thankfulness and love are founded on *daily* choices. I'm committed to do whatever I can to make Darell's life easier and more enjoyable on any given day. When I'm frustrated because I want to go out to a place in the evening but I know Darell does better if he's in bed by eight o'clock, I embrace the opportunity to help him instead of fixating on what it's costing me. I have a chance to serve my husband. I have a chance to make his life better. Those little choices make me a more thankful person, even though I'm the one doing the serving.

Darell helps by cultivating an attitude of appreciation. He doesn't slip into a "woe is me" mode. Les and Leslie Parrott warn that "self-pity is the luxury no marriage can afford. It's guaranteed to drain all the energy from you and your relationship. Any amount of self-pity is more than enough."[5]

Darell also doesn't take it for granted that Stacy, as his wife, is "supposed" to make sacrifices like this. "Stacy's care for me is always going to be a duty, but my response can turn it into a delight."

Stacy wants to serve Darell because she delights in his well-being. Darell appreciates Stacy's service and works hard to make sure her service is delightful to her. They can't change the situation, but they have learned how to use a terrible situation to delight in each other. Thus, the terrible situation is making their marriage stronger, not weaker.

That's real faith applied!

> The Lord is good,
>> a refuge in times of trouble.
> He cares for those who trust in him. (Nahum 1:7)

Building Your Fortress Takeaways

1. To succeed in marriage, we must succeed in learning how to mentally manage loss. If we don't learn to turn disappointment into determination, helplessness into hope, and frustration into faith, our marriage won't go far in a hostile world.

2. Spouses frequently respond to fears and the death of expectations in different ways. Intimacy is strengthened when we learn from each other instead of automatically assuming that our response is the healthiest response.

3. Unaddressed fears often come out as hurtful secondary emotions, so it's important to courageously address your fears as fear so you can talk about it.

4. Responding in a healthy way to your spouse's fears requires "differentiation"—understanding and bearing your spouse's frustrations and disappointments without making it about you.

5. Talking about your fears shouldn't be seen as *blaming* your spouse; it's *helping* your spouse understand you so that the two of you can face your disappointment together.

6. When dreams die in marriage, each spouse needs a different spiritual prescription. The "spiritual medicine" that heals you may not help your spouse.

7. After you name your fear, accept the reality of the new situation. Denial only makes things worse. You need to live and relate to each other accordingly.

8. Christian transformation begins with the mind. To face your own disappointments, you need enlightenment, which includes a greater understanding of yourself. What is this trial teaching you about you?

9. In classical Christian teaching, surrender is the humble acknowledgment that life works better when we adopt God's agenda over our own and learn what he wants us to learn instead of trying to convince God that what we initially wanted is best.

10. Sometimes our fears of a potential problem do as much damage if not more damage than the problem itself.

11. One of the best tools for growth is learning how to grieve in a healthy way.

12. While grieving is important, we will thrive when we also learn to celebrate consistently and persistently what we still have instead of fixating on what we've lost.

13. The Bible urges us to pray for healing, but we should also pray for grace.

CHAPTER 2

THE "UNMATCHABLE" CONNECTION

Fighting to Keep Your Marriage Close

I've worked with and talked to a lot of couples, but there's just something about Debra and John that makes them seem like a couple's couple. They're together, in every sense of the word. They're *one*. Even though they've been married just fifteen years, they have a mature unity that's inspiring.

They're happy together (cue the Turtles' 1967 massive hit).

Which is all the more surprising given that they have four children, including, as I write this, a baby. There were moments when their marriage had to adjust to fit in each child, but by baby number four, Debra believes they have it down. "At the end of the day, I'm more obsessed with my husband by baby number four than I've ever been before. So something is working!"

Doesn't that sound wonderful—each new child *increasing* your intimacy with each other instead of getting in the way? It doesn't have to be about raising children, of course. It could be handling an increased workload, caring for a sick parent, surviving April if one of you is an accountant, getting through a full moon if you're an obstetrician, or keeping your marriage together at Christmas and Easter if you're a pastor.

The primary danger this chapter addresses, regardless of the particular marital challenge you're facing, is marital *disconnection*. Christian psychologists Dr. Archibald Hart and Dr. Sharon May warn, "The hurt and pain that come from being emotionally disconnected for many years can leave deep scars of loneliness, unhappiness, and disappointment."[6] Putting up with disconnection for any serious length of time becomes an assault on your marriage.

Drs. Les and Leslie Parrott point out that when you give birth to a new child, you're also giving birth to a new marriage: "Studies show that when baby makes three, conflicts increase eightfold, marriage takes a backseat, women feel overburdened, and men feel shoved aside . . . In the year after the first baby arrives, 70 percent of wives experience a precipitous plummet in their marital satisfaction. For the husband, the dissatisfaction usually kicks in later, as a reaction to his wife's unhappiness."[7]

You know what else creates a new marriage? A health crisis. An empty nest. A drug-addicted child. A change in employment. Debra and John's increasing intimacy with the addition of each child, as opposed to the more typical increasing distance with each child, isn't an accident. They've been thoughtful and intentional about staying emotionally connected. Let's see what we can learn from them and what you can apply, regardless of what threatens to tear you apart.

EARLY LOVE

Debra is a licensed professional counselor; John is an eye surgeon. The road to both occupations is arduous and time-consuming, yet from the very start, Debra and John learned to make their relationship a priority.

"Before we had kids, I think I'd most describe our marriage as intimate and fun," John remembers. "We went for a lot of walks and slept in really late. Both of us are full-blooded Egyptians, so . . ."

"That means when we went to the Sunday 11:00 service, we got up at 10:45," Debra says, finishing his sentence with a laugh.

"What I remember most," John continues, "is being free to stay up until 1:00 a.m., connect with each other throughout the day, do things together, and basically just explore life and whatever community we lived in."

"We were free!" Debra adds. "Even when John was in medical school, it didn't feel busy because we didn't have kids. I was finishing up my practicum and internship, but compared to now, I definitely don't feel like it was a busy season. Some people say the first year of marriage is the hardest; that's not even close to true for us."

They appeared ideally positioned to face the sometimes intimacy-challenging beginning of child-rearing. But for a while, even this unusually well-matched couple felt like life was trying to rip apart the seams of their marriage.

AND BABY MAKES THREE

Debra and John had been married for three years when their first daughter came along.

"It was a major change right from the start," John remembers. "Just drastically different. On top of Deb having a new baby, we moved to a new city and I started residency."

It didn't help that their daughter wasn't exactly a "cherub." "She was a little drill sergeant," Debra laughs, "who wanted everything to revolve around her. I literally felt like I was on house arrest for a season.

"Oh, and John was working a hundred hours a week in residency, which meant I felt like a single mom. He was on call almost all the time and only had four days off a month."

Further adding to their challenge, Debra went through postpartum depression. "I didn't know what it was at the time, but hormonally I was completely messed up. And John is sort of like Mister Rogers optimistic. He didn't know what to do with me. Eventually, his tactic of dealing with my depression was to withdraw, which is not at all what I needed or wanted."

Sexual intimacy, which had been a valued and enjoyable part of their relationship, became something of a stranger. John attributes some of his withdrawal to sheer weariness. "I had interest in intimacy but not much energy for intimacy. All the pictures we have of me that year are me lying down sleeping with the baby on top of me."

It was hard for Debra not to take some of this personally. "The manuals always say the man usually initiates sex, but John definitely was not initiating, so it made me feel even worse. I'm reading all these books about how he's 'supposed' to be that way, so when he wasn't and I was already feeling depressed, it made me feel even worse. It was a really bad combination."

Debra's former default mode of thinking is a common but devastating one. We take something universal and make it personal.

It's understandable why we do that, but it never helps. Working one-hundred-hour weeks will dampen the sexual ardor of just about anyone. John's disinterest, though hurtful, wasn't a reflection of Debra being undesirable; it was simply a reflection of him being tired.

I've heard it said, "Make the situation your enemy instead of your spouse."*

I talked to a wife in charge of her company's tech needs. Their system crashed during a busy season, and she had executives above her and colleagues below her screaming out their frustration about how they couldn't get anything done until she got the system back up and running. She knew her husband was feeling ignored as she worked nights and weekends, but her workmates screamed louder than he did.

Her husband could have recognized her panic and showed empathy and understanding. Instead, he felt hurt and neglected, only adding to her stress, and then he ended up getting into an emotional affair. He took personally what was happening. Pride got in the way, which is what happens when we take what our spouse is going through and make it a statement about us rather than seeking to understand, support, and encourage our spouse.

Becoming hyperaware of our own hurt and frustration can blind us to the hurt and frustration our spouse is going through. I'm not talking about abusive situations in which a spouse needs to seek safety rather than understanding. If you don't feel safe, you can't connect emotionally. I'm talking about self-focus and self-obsession that make us so aware of our own lot in life that we have no mental space to have empathy for our spouse. The apostle Paul

---

* I'm sorry I don't know the actual genesis of this quote. It was suggested to me by a friend, and I've held on to it. And my friend didn't know where she heard it either.

urges believers to counter this "self first" approach to life when he tells us to "do nothing out of selfish ambition or vain conceit. Rather, in humility value others above yourselves, not looking to your own interests but each of you to the interests of the others" (Philippians 2:3–4). This isn't a onetime teaching of Paul's, by the way. Consider 1 Corinthians 10:24: "No one should seek their own good, but the good of others."

Spiritual maturity means learning to think of others first. Spiritual maturity means defaulting to curiosity before condemnation, empathy before judgment, and care before censure. Marriage is one of the best training grounds for learning how to adopt this attitude.

Allowing emotional disconnection to continue is hazardous to your marriage. Drs. Hart and May define distressed marriages as "those where spouses are no longer emotionally connected in a secure and loving way."[8] Disconnection is distress. Admit it, but don't put up with it.

WITHDRAWING FROM WITHDRAWAL

Dr. John Gottman calls withdrawal—something John was doing in his marriage—one of the "four horsemen of the apocalypse," relationally speaking.* And, interestingly enough, he says that most stonewallers (his overall term for withdrawers) are men. Withdrawal can sound passive, but it's actively destructive. Gottman lists stonewalling, especially when women stonewall, as a fairly reliable predictor of divorce.[9]

Let's look at why withdrawal didn't doom John and Debra to

---

* For the "four horsemen" image, see Revelation 6:1–8.

THE "UNMATCHABLE" CONNECTION

this fate. When stonewalling arises, it is often reinforced by what Gottman calls "emotional flooding."[10] The husband feels overwhelmed with his wife's concerns and verbal attacks. Gottman warns in particular about "harsh start-ups—when the wife (though it's not always the wife) responds to the husband's withdrawal by beginning the conversation in a harsh manner, with words that are immediate, hot, loud, intense, and sharp."[11]

"You never listen to me!"

"You prioritize everything but me!"

"You never pay attention to me!"

Statements like these put the other spouse on the defensive. An emotionally connected couple feels safe; a spouse under attack naturally wants to defend themselves. *If your spouse doesn't feel safe with you, they can't feel intimate with you.* If your marriage isn't a place of security, it will never be a place of emotional connection.

Before you express your anger, express your love. Before you express your disappointment, express your overwhelming desire to be close to each other. Instead of saying, "How could you do this to me?" say, "I love you so much, and I'm scared that we're drifting apart," or "I really miss you," or "I hate how this challenge is pulling us apart."

Think *safety*. Think *connection*. These are the two "pedals" of marriage that will help you ride back together. Harsh words, verbal attacks, and sullen silence take a bad situation and make it worse. As the proverb writer says, "A gentle answer turns away wrath, but a harsh word stirs up anger" (Proverbs 15:1). Learn how to feel grief and pain and yet talk with invitation and empathy: "Let your conversation be always full of grace, seasoned with salt, so that you may know how to answer everyone" (Colossians 4:6).

Hart and May explain: "What the research does show is that

fighting—and by this we mean arguments and disagreements, not physical encounters—is not necessarily hazardous to a marriage . . . John Gottman's research found that it wasn't the content of arguments that predicted divorce, but the *emotional disengagement* that accompanies these fights . . . As long as couples remain emotionally connected, their marriages can survive until they find a way around their differences."[12]

THE TURNAROUND

After stumbling along for a few months, Debra started to feel a little better as her hormones gradually returned to normal levels. That gave her enough energy to examine their marriage with more insight and perspective.

"Something had to give. John couldn't work less and we couldn't return the baby, so that left me as the remaining link to create something different. I had to adjust something."

I love Debra's attitude. It's so easy during difficult seasons of marriage to start to feel sorry for ourselves, which only makes us feel worse, which further depletes our energy, which causes things to slip a little further in the wrong direction, which reinforces our discouragement, and so on. In her books and counseling practice, Debra preaches *active resistance* and *God-inspired initiation.* Instead of just passively letting things happen, we need to take charge, with God's help, and work to find a way through, leaning on this promise: "I am the LORD your God who takes hold of your right hand and says to you, Do not fear; I will help you" (Isaiah 41:13). Life isn't easy, so sometimes we need to lean into the Spirit's

* To learn more about Debra's books and ministry, visit www.truelovedates.com.

comfort and assistance to confront what's off-kilter and give our marriage another try.

Every marriage that maintains long-term emotional connection is a marriage in which, during various seasons, one partner had to take the first step. One partner had to temporarily carry more of the load.

Part of John and Debra's marital recovery meant that John had to learn how to help Debra cope with her depression. Some women in Debra's situation might have resented their husbands' withdrawal, but most men don't have a psychology degree. Most people don't know how to identify depression or don't know what to do even if there has been a diagnosis. Expecting your spouse to understand and have the right response ready just because they love you isn't realistic. Explaining to your spouse what's going on and then talking together about how to address it is the best way to make your marriage a fortress.

Eventually, Debra and John's marriage came back together. The experience of postpartum depression actually increased their intimacy because it forced them to face and overcome something new, something they had to face as a couple, not just as individuals.

If you're the spouse working crazy hours or the spouse staying home, or if both of you are trying to return to work as soon as possible after a baby is born—no matter what your situation is—face it *as a couple*. Talk about it *as a couple*. Both of you may feel like you're drowning, but it's vital to learn how to swim out of it together. Isolation creates a third problem, which may become an even bigger challenge than what led to the isolation in the first place. Independently "gritting your teeth and bearing it" can result in resentment and emotional separation.

Admit that it's difficult for both of you. Admit that both of you feel shortchanged. Admit that neither one of you seems to be having all that much fun. Instead of resenting each other, pursue empathy for each other. If your spouse is experiencing depression, you can even say, "I'm sorry you're going through this. I don't know how to help, but I want to. Tell me what would help you the most in this season." Even if you feel like you never signed up for this and have a spouse who is completely different from the one you married, an empathetic response is what's needed. Whatever you do, don't make it "me versus you." *You can be frustrated with your spouse and feel empathy for your spouse at the same time.* In fact, a successful, intimate marriage will require you to do just that.

If you've never had children before (or multiple children at the same time), you can't fault yourself or each other for not knowing what to do the first time around. In whatever season you and your spouse are in, let the uncertainty and the search for solutions become a glue that binds you ever closer together.

ROUND TWO

Baby number two didn't present quite the same challenge to Debra and John's marriage as did baby number one. For starters, Debra was wise enough to get on medication for her postpartum depression right away. "As a counselor, part of me thinks I should be able to talk myself through this, but you can't. If you need medication, take your medication." Maturity is holistic; sometimes you may not be facing a marital issue so much as a medical issue.

For his part, John awakened to the reality that raising kids is a lot of work. He already knew that, but now he was prepared to face it head-on. You can't just add a new baby into your life as if there were a gaping hole of time and energy waiting to be filled. Something has to give, and John was already working at near maximum capacity. So what *do* you do? You realize where you fell short the first time and then prepare in advance for what's to come. John couldn't feel bad about being caught off guard by the addition of the first baby, but he could certainly anticipate the same thing (and more) happening when the second baby came.

I've had to do this as a writer. It may seem obvious, but since I don't use ghostwriters, if I don't write, books don't get written. I also don't preach other preachers' sermons. So some seasons of preaching and writing can get quite taxing. In the midst of this, family events still happen. One summer I was facing a publishing deadline and a long sermon series (six out of seven weeks) at church, with three conferences sprinkled in between. My wife scheduled a family vacation in the middle of all this because it fit into our adult children's schedules.

Because I've been buried by things like this before, I knew what not to do: keep my normal schedule and hope that "God's grace" would carry me through my lack of preparation when the roof collapsed. Instead, I worked like crazy *ahead of time*, planning sermons and working on the book long before that season arrived. I anticipated the crunch and tried to make it a little less of a crunch. April is always going to be extremely busy for a tax accountant in the United States, but eventually the accountant can learn how to make their marriage work by looking at what doesn't work, anticipating what will need to be done, and addressing it relationally and vocationally before everything falls apart. Maybe they take on one less client. Maybe they add part-time help. There will be financial costs but huge relational gains. *Something* has to give, and for that, choose what is least important.

In addition to staying ahead of the challenge, we also have to re-evaluate our priorities. John says, "I realized the reality of our family situation. Though I needed to catch up on sleep, I still had to be a husband and dad and put in the work at home, not just the work at the hospital."

"He had to work on not just giving us the leftovers," Debra adds.

"When I came home, I had to remind myself that even though I felt like I needed a break or some sleep or just a half hour to unwind, the reality is you can't put your family on pause. I had to choose a more selfless route. Especially when I walked in the door, the first five minutes are the most important to Debra. Do I show her I'm interested? Do I ask about her day? I had to learn to be deliberate in my focus as soon as I got home."

You may not find a solution that doesn't hurt. A God-honoring life involves sacrifice. Jesus said, on more than one occasion, that if we want to follow him, a cross will be involved (see Matthew 16:24–26; Luke 9:23). Paul said the Christian life is about continually offering up our bodies as *living* sacrifices (see Romans 12:1). In my experience in pastoral counseling, many couples want a solution that has no pain associated with it. They want to stay connected without losing anything that has been keeping them so busy, distracted, and disconnected. Let me be blunt: When you add a baby to your life, you have to take something out. When you add a serious season of grieving in your life (the death of a parent, friend, or sibling), something needs to be taken out. We don't get more hours, so we need to subtract from what fills those hours. Otherwise, our "crises" will drive us apart.

BOUNDARIES

I mentioned earlier in the chapter that it isn't an accident that John and Debra drew closer together as they raised small children. They are wonderfully intense about setting and keeping boundaries. As a friend, I have always admired and respected this about Debra, but she says, "If you think I'm assertive, you haven't met John."

If you let life push you around as individuals, the world is going to push you apart as a couple. Debra and John both understood this danger early on and told themselves, "That's not going to happen to us."

Debra explains, "One of the themes in our marriage is the word *no*. We learned very quickly that if we were going to survive and do well as a couple and family, we had to say no to anything and anyone that could get in the way of our family and marriage. That remains true to this day, even if saying no involves a kid."

Their boundaries included not letting the kids sleep in their room. "We made a wise investment in sleep training so that all of our kids learned how to sleep in their crib without needing Mom and Dad on a regular basis. We focused on teaching the kids this early on so John and I could protect our own relationship.

"The kids all know that when the door is closed, they can't come in Mommy and Daddy's room. This is *our* sanctuary, and it's *our* time. We're not available anymore."

Debra holds to this policy without apology. "Some people think it's mean to set boundaries with your kids like that, but if you don't take care of your marriage, you won't have anything left over to give the kids."

SUNDAY NIGHT CHECK-INS

In spite of putting in place strong boundaries and seeking renewed understanding in their marriage, Debra and John still struggled somewhat after bringing home baby number two. Even if you know what to do, if you don't do it fully, your marriage is going to suffer. You can recognize what went wrong, but then you have to adapt if the old solution isn't working.

Thus began Debra and John's Sunday night "check-ins."

We were struggling in our marriage. At the worst point, we needed to check in every Sunday night. It was intentional and deliberate: How are we doing, what are we struggling with, what does the other person need, what complaints do we need to air? We have literally been doing this every Sunday night since.

Having these check-ins is a priority, no matter where they are—whether they're traveling or at home, on vacation or meeting deadlines.

Another couple, Rebekah and Rod, do nightly debriefs:

Every night before we go to sleep, we ask each other three questions: When did you feel loved by me today? When did you feel respected by me today? Did I hurt you? After doing your *Cherish* study, we started throwing in various questions about when we felt cherished. This keeps everything out in the light. We tend to address hurt right away so we don't have to deal with it in bed. We don't shove anything under the rug, which was part of the demise of our first marriages. Plus, we give each other plenty of material to work with so we know what we can do to fill each other's love buckets.

For Debra and John, the check-ins became particularly important to them because they believed back then and still believe now that in certain seasons, "date nights" are completely unrealistic. "Sometimes trying to have date nights caused more problems than it solved," says Debra. "You make grand plans but the kids get sick, or the babysitter needs you to come back in the middle of it, or something happened during the week so you don't have money and can't afford it."

So for the most part, the check-ins are done at home. "We set up our schedule so the kids go to bed earlier, at 8:30 or 9:00, and John and I are always up until midnight or later, and that's *our* time."

This schedule gives them two to three hours of alone time every night. They may watch something on Netflix, be intimate, read books, or play chess together. They take time to talk about their walks with the Lord, pray together, and share what they're learning.

Parenting decisions routinely test the boundaries of a couple's alone time. "Some parents parent out of guilt," says Debra. "They feel guilty saying no to their kids, but I believe that learning to say no to your kids is an important part of having a healthy marriage."

John backs this up. "Our kids don't get to participate in several activities at once. In fact, they get to choose just one. Otherwise, with four children, four nights out of the week we'll be away from home. We're not going to get distracted. None of our kids are going to play professional sports, so we're not going to let that remote possibility obliterate our family schedule."

"Our friends call us essentialists," Debra says with a laugh.

It doesn't appear at all that she wants to reject that label.

Debra and John know it's unusual for a couple to have up to three hours of alone time every night. For some couples, that may not be possible. Yet they are firm believers that "if you don't have time for just the two of you, it's impossible to invest in your marriage." Marriage, conversation, and intimacy all take time. If you don't protect that time, whether it's three hours or thirty minutes, you can't build your marriage, your friendship, or your sex life.

Boundaries are not about making your kids suffer for the sake of the marriage. On the contrary, boundaries around your alone time make your marriage prosper for the benefit of your kids. Debra explains, "Your kids need you to have a good marriage. What you model to them is the best way for your kids to learn about future healthy relationships."

John and Debra want their kids to grow up in a home where Mom and Dad kiss each other regularly, touch each other, hug each other, and occasionally have arguments but then are quick to apologize. "We want to raise our kids out of the fullness of our marriage instead of the emptiness of our marriage."

GROWING APART BY NOT INTENTIONALLY GROWING TOGETHER

Modern life isn't a lake; it's a river. If you're not paddling somewhere, you're being carried downstream. That's especially true of marriage—and even truer when you're married with small children (or have teenagers).

Debra counsels, "I think the biggest problem I see when I'm working with couples is that the husband says, 'She's changed,' or the wife says, 'We've grown apart.' Of course that will happen if you're not keeping up with each other! It's your job to stay connected."

If you don't have a plan to stay connected and vigorously protect that plan, you won't stay connected.

John adds, "We've been really deliberate since we got married about everything, even our hobbies. In the especially busy years, we had zero hobbies. There was no bandwidth left for either of us to have a hobby, but now we go for walks, take hikes, or go on bike rides. We're determined to use our free time to draw closer instead of drift further away, which is why I don't join the other doctors who go golfing for six hours without their wives."

"I wouldn't let him even if he wanted to!" Debra chimes in.

I heard my wife, Lisa, recently tell someone, "Gary has more close male friends than any man I've ever met," but she's speaking of me as an empty nester. When our kids were young, I worked, wrote, went to church, and spent time with the family. I didn't really have time to have a thirty-minute conversation with a buddy on the West Coast or to meet up with my young hipster, guitar-playing friend at Pondicheri for dinner. Looking back, I don't regret that. The celebrated author and theologian Elton Trueblood taught me that life is lived in chapters, so I urge you to be responsible to the chapter you're writing. That chapter doesn't have to define you for life, just this season of your life. You can establish other priorities as you complete one chapter and turn to the next. What you don't want to do is try to write five chapters at once and come out with five failures.

RECOGNIZING YOUR LIMITS

I'm a big fan of the Tour de France and have read several autobiographies of past winners. One of the things that astonishes me most about modern bicycling is the level of self-discipline required to maintain a light weight. These guys are freaks of nature—they have the quadriceps of an offensive lineman, the calves of an Olympic gymnast, and the biceps of a chess player. One champion biker wouldn't carry a bag of groceries into his house because he didn't want to add any weight to his arms. If that sounds extreme, you've never watched someone *pedal* themselves to the top of Alpe d'Huez. These guys will empty their water bottles at the base of a climb just to shed an ounce or two of weight.

Geraint Thomas, the 2018 winner of the Tour de France, put it simply: "Professional bikers don't eat ice creams." Their body weight must be optimal. Every calorie they consume has to produce energy without creating excess fat. It is as difficult for a man to maintain a biker's body as it is for an aging ballerina to maintain a dancer's body. All of nature seems to work against it.

Maintaining an intimate marriage while having kids requires the same kind of discipline. You can lose the race to the top of Alpe d'Huez before you ever clip your shoes into your pedals if you're not disciplined outside of the "race." Do you want to eat ice cream, or do you want to quickly climb giant mountains on a bike? You can't do both.

In the same way, something is going to have to give if you want your marriage to remain intimate. You might be able to stay *married* while ignoring your schedule and level of energy, but you can't stay *intimate*. Part of what is required is an honest assessment.

"John has a smaller emotional bandwidth than I do," Debra

explains. "After seeing forty-five to fifty patients a day, he has spent 75 percent of his energy."

That's why—get ready for this—John works only three days a week. And his office is only five minutes from home. He also usually eats lunch at home.

"We figured out what works for us. Some people can't do that, but you have to learn to adapt and change and evolve in the season you're in. We live below our means so we can make family a priority. That means I drive a fifteen-year-old car. I've made decisions to gain financial freedom."

Debra says, "The natural trajectory of marriage is drift; that's what is going to happen, like in the ocean. Drift is what you should expect in marriage instead of being surprised by it. The whole goal of lifestyle choices is how do you fight the drift? If you do nothing and take a passive stance, drift is going to happen. And you can't rest. You have to constantly adopt an active approach. The more kids you have, the more drift happens because there are so many different things to navigate.

"One of the biggest traps is assuming this is just a season and you don't have to put in the work right now," Debra adds. "Well, this season may pass, but so will your marriage."

THE PAYOFF

As John and Debra put all of these principles into action, adding child number three was actually easier for them than adding child number two. And adding child number four was the easiest of all.

John explains, "By trial and error, we figured it out. We know how to take care of the baby and keep our priorities set to the point where we just fit him into our schedule instead of letting him run our schedule. To be honest, though we didn't expect this fourth child, he hasn't really interrupted us all that much."

Debra adds, "That's because we're a team, we take turns, we help each other, and we've figured out our own rhythm. Plus, we've become really good at telling each other what we need. Communication makes marriage a lot easier."

This may sound like a lot of work, but consider this: While Geraint Thomas made a lot of sacrifices to win the 2018 Tour de France, if you saw the joy on his face after the time trial in stage 20 in which he knew the yellow jersey was safely his forever, it was clear he wasn't missing the "ice creams." He had found something much better.

John explains what comes from unashamedly setting boundaries, making financial sacrifices, and locking the bedroom door during lovemaking. "When you can live in that freedom, the level of intimacy is unmatchable. You will experience unbelievable love, connection, support, and sexual intimacy that is better than you imagined and more frequent than most guys could hope for. Even more, you feel like you're doing what God is calling you to do, and you have the tremendous satisfaction of knowing your kids are growing up in that kind of healthy environment."

Debra adds, "My motto has always been that healthy people make healthy relationships, especially in marriage. As you focus on your primary relationship, figuring out what you need to keep your marriage growing strong, there will be a healthy overflow into all of your other relationships. When people subvert this and rely on their kids to fill their emotional needs, it causes a lot of long-term damage."

John points to another benefit of making our marriage

a fortress by making it the best it can be. "When you are fully exposed and known and don't have anything to hide and your spouse still accepts you, there is nothing better than that feeling. If someone were to ask me where I find my greatest happiness—in being a successful surgeon or in having a connected family—it's not even a contest. Being connected to your wife and kids is way better. It comes down to what is your identity. When people ask about me, I don't tell them I'm an eye surgeon. That's just my day job. My identity is, I'm married to Deb and have four kids."

> Taste and see that the LORD is good;
> blessed is the one who takes refuge in him.
> (Psalm 34:8)

Building Your Fortress Takeaways

1. Emotional disconnection leads to marital disconnection, which can leave "deep scars of loneliness, unhappiness, and disappointment."
2. Giving birth to a new child is like giving birth to a new marriage.
3. When you're in a busy or difficult season, try to resent the *situation* instead of resenting your *spouse*.
4. According to Drs. Hart and May, distressed marriages are "those where spouses are no longer emotionally connected in a secure and loving way."

5. Withdrawal and stonewalling are brutally destructive to a marriage.

6. If your spouse doesn't feel safe with you, they can't feel intimate with you. If your marriage isn't a place of security, it will never be a place of emotional connection.

7. Self-obsession and the refusal to sacrifice lead to immaturity as a believer and disconnection as a couple.

8. Instead of giving up when attachment becomes difficult, practice *active resistance* and *God-inspired initiation*. Every marriage that maintains long-term emotional connection is a marriage in which, during various seasons, one partner had to take the first step.

9. Face your challenge as a couple. Isolation creates a third problem, which may become an even bigger challenge than what led to the isolation in the first place.

10. You can be frustrated with your spouse and feel empathy for your spouse at the same time. In fact, a successful, intimate marriage will require you to do just that.

11. You need to set priorities and not put family life on pause.

12. If you let life push you around as individuals, the world is going to push you apart as a couple.

13. Weekly check-ins or even nightly debriefs are valuable tools to stay connected.

14. If you don't *plan* to stay connected and then vigorously *protect* that plan, you won't stay connected.

CHAPTER 3

WHEN DISTANCE DOESN'T MATTER

Growing Together Even While Spending Time Apart

A s Navy chaplain Baron Miller ushered me into his quarters in Guantanamo Bay, I noticed a cardboard cutout of his face and shoulders hanging up in the garage.

"What's that?" I asked.

"That's Flat Baron," he said with a laugh. His wife, Cristina, used the cardboard cutout as a stand-in for Baron when he was away on assignment, a creative way to remind his family that he was there for them in spirit even when he wasn't there in body.

As a naval chaplain, Baron has spent more than two years being separated from Cristina and his family. They have learned it is foolish and dangerous to just "hope" that physical distance won't tear them apart as a couple. Instead, they believe couples must learn how to grow their relationship even when they live on different continents.

If one of you travels for business of any kind or you have to be away for a season to care for an ailing parent, and certainly if you are in the military, their story will inspire you. Yet even if you're never apart (my parents haven't spent two successive days apart in more than sixty years of marriage), the principles behind Cristina and Baron's intentional pursuit of intimacy will be encouraging and instructive.

A NEW NORMAL

"We never spent more than a week apart until I joined the Navy," Baron says. "The night before I flew out to officer development school was daunting. I was going to be gone for five weeks. It was the saddest moment ever, with the kids crying and Cristina worried, and I kept saying to myself, *What have I done?*"

Officer development school was just the start. A few months after returning home, Baron entered chaplain school, which lasts for eight weeks. In time, separations became a regular part of their lives. Within one year of his graduation from chaplaincy school, Baron was in Afghanistan. Further deployments usually lasted 90 to 180 days, "except for Special Ops, which were usually just three-week trips" (but especially dangerous, of course).

EXPECTATIONS

It took a few tries for Baron and Cristina to learn to reconnect in a healthy and seamless way. They soon learned that both spouses needed to be more honest and explicit about their expectations. If there was just one piece of advice I'd give to traveling couples, it would be along these lines: *The spouse who travels should be open and up-front about their hopes for what kind of environment they are going to walk back into. And the spouse who stays at home should be equally open and up-front about what they need on their end.*

Frankly, this is good advice even if you're talking about a normal workday separation of ten hours. Couples could spare themselves a lot of grief if they'd just talk about reentry.

If you've never traveled, you don't know what it's like to come home from a long trip—having battled weariness, temptations, a sense of longing and loneliness. If you've never been the one to stay home, you don't know what it's like to hang on until the spouse returns—the weariness, temptations, frustration, monotonous routines, aloneness.

Both of you will likely feel very alone during the time of separation. Learn how to face your aloneness together. A little communication can go a long way. Actively seek to understand what it is about the separation that's most difficult for your spouse.

When our own children were young, Lisa was adamant about making sure the house was clean when I got home because that's the kind of home she'd like to return to. But I don't really notice dishes in the sink. I don't inspect counters for crumbs. Instead, I hated coming home to the sound of a vacuum cleaner. Lisa thought the "sound of cleaning" was the "sound of music," a sure sign that she loved me. I was usually exhausted and craved peace and tranquility.

It was the opposite for Cristina and Baron, which is why couples need to talk about this. There isn't one right answer. Cristina explains, "Baron expected that things would be taken care of while he was gone in the same way they were taken care of when he was home. The problem is, when he was home, there were *two* parents helping out, not one, so that expectation wasn't realistic with little kids. He had to adjust his expectations."

Baron wanted the house clean, and he admits that his earlier stint as an enlisted Marine gave him a "military grade" definition of clean. "Cristina would excitedly share how she cleaned the car before I got home, but I saw that the steering wheel was sticky. When I pointed it out and she countered with, 'Well, I vacuumed it but forgot to wash the steering wheel,' I appreciated the sentiment, but that explanation wouldn't fly in the military. Clean is clean, and a sticky steering wheel isn't clean. I *do* blame the Marine Corps for that definition of clean, by the way."

Baron also preferred for the house to stay the same as when he left. He didn't want the furniture rearranged or even the art on the wall to be moved. He was agreeable to Cristina asking him to help move furniture around after he got back, but there was just something meaningful to him about coming back to a familiar place.

The first time Cristina moved the furniture a little bit or changed a picture, she had no idea how much it would bother Baron. She couldn't have known, until he told her why, and then she understood. All of us have expectations that our spouses can never guess. So talk about them. And then talk some more.

IF SOMETHING BUGS YOU, IT BUGS YOU, SO TALK ABOUT IT

A lack of communication is the most typical failure when couples suffer from separations. In many cases, both spouses feel their own set of agitations—the one who travels feels guilty about being gone; the spouse who stays home feels taken advantage of because they have to fulfill the duties of both parents while the other spouse is away. If something bugs you, it bugs you—and you need to talk about it.

Baron learned how important speaking up was. "At first, I stuffed the irritation down until I couldn't stuff it down anymore, and then it didn't come out very tactfully." Travel is synonymous with stress—and remember, a different kind of stress for each spouse. One spouse is tired from being on the road; the other spouse is tired from parenting alone, managing the household duties on their own, or even missing out on the new experiences the traveling spouse has enjoyed while they've been cooped up in the same old apartment or house. If you don't choose to talk about your stress and expectations when you're in a good place (i.e., not right when you walk in the door), you're more likely to verbally explode when you're in a not-so-good place.

Recognizing this, Cristina and Baron's second deployment (Baron left one year later to go to Spain and Africa) went much better, in large part because they talked about their expectations *before* Baron left. Baron summarized it this way:

> Our goal for the first deployment was to depart well because that was all we knew. Our goal for the second deployment was to depart well *and return well*. Cristina was also honest about how difficult it was to keep things clean when she was the only parent in the house, so I made sure she knew I didn't care if we paid somebody to help her out. We made the choice that a clean house was worth the cost. We were buying a more peaceful return for me and less stress for Cristina while I was away, and it was worth every penny we paid.

Let's say you never travel longer than eight hours—that is, you and/or your spouse come home from work every night. Or your spouse works late and comes home after you've fed the kids and put them to bed. My friend Mary Kay, who speaks to a lot of women's groups, points out, "Sometimes it is easier to cope with a husband being away than him working late. If he is away, the wife knows the evening is hers after the kids are in bed. If he works late, he expects attention to be on him after she has already done everything else by herself."

Regardless of your particular situation, you can still apply these principles. What kind of environment do you want to come home to after a stressful day at the office? (Men, listen to Shania Twain's hit song "Honey, I'm Home" to get an idea of what at least one working woman wants!) How do you want the out-of-the house spouse to act when they walk through the door? And how does the stay-at-home spouse want to be welcomed? This is equally and maybe even *especially* true if both of you work. Unexpressed expectations don't cease to be expectations; they just become a breeding ground for resentment and bitterness. Stuffing things down because they feel selfish is like growing a swamp of mosquitoes in your master bedroom. Drain the swamp by talking about what you want. Both of you may have to compromise, but do so with your expectations out in the open.

One of the ways I failed as a husband who traveled a lot was never sharing my expectations with Lisa. I thought the "holy" response was to ignore the inconveniences I felt and try to see everything from her perspective. But that robbed Lisa of wanting to be more welcoming, and the natural intimacy that would follow (I'm not talking about sex; I'm talking about her feeling cherished and prized). There are many things she now wishes she would have done differently, but she never knew about my expectations. I was wrong not to communicate better. In retrospect, my silence robbed our relationship rather than served it.

It's not a sin to advocate for yourself. It is a sin to selfishly demand your way and to only consider your own desires without regard to your spouse's welfare and needs. Expressing your desires and preferences in an attitude of cooperation and intimacy is healthy and will lead to growth in your marriage. Self-proclaimed "martyrs" can produce a lot of misery in their marriage in the name of godliness, but it's sometimes a proud piety more than a true holiness. Jesus is the holiest person who ever lived, yet he allowed women to support him financially (Luke 8:1–3). He allowed a family to give him a dinner in his honor (John 12:2). He let Peter "earn" and then pay his taxes (Matthew 17:24–27). He allowed a woman to anoint him with oil (Luke 7:36–50). And he even allowed a man to carry his cross on the way to Golgotha (Matthew 27:31–32).

KEEPING IN TOUCH

Baron realized you can't make up for a long absence with one grand gesture (or one big gift), so he got creative about staying connected on a near daily basis, as much as he could. Before he left for one deployment, he purchased five hundred postcards—some for Cristina, "princess" ones for his daughter, and cartoon ones for his son. Because military mail can be sporadic, Baron sometimes wrote a dozen in a single day, and Cristina would space out their delivery. The postcards often contained nothing more than a few sentences: that he was thinking of them, what he loved about each of them, what he was hoping to do when he got back.

"My goal was to do a postcard a day for all three of them."

Writing daily postcards wasn't easy. As a deployed chaplain, Baron is honest about the drudgery. "You have nothing new to say. It's the same war, everything is still dirty, everything is still brown. And while the names of those who get injured or die might change, you can't write about that."

Some of the postcards to Cristina were adult-oriented. They could be "sexual" as a couple, even though they were on different continents (more on this later).

Another thing they did was to think through how to make the limited verbal contact as meaningful as possible. Baron says:

> We settled on high/low. What was the best part of your day, and what was the worst? Sometimes by the time I got back into base, I'd be toast. My mind was so occupied by the events of the day, and the time zones were sometimes difficult to navigate.
>
> What I loved about high/low is that it helped Cristina focus. If I simply asked her how her day had gone, she could inundate me with so much minutiae that it was hard, with a fatigued brain, to stay with her. I wouldn't just hear, "I talked to Sally"; I'd hear, "I talked to Sally and she ordered that salad I like but tried a different dressing, and you wouldn't *believe* what just happened between her and so-and-so . . ." She'd give me a full account of literally *everything* they talked about. I didn't want to cut her off, but I also had limited energy, so when we focused the conversation on the best part of each other's day, it became more manageable.

For the more talkative spouse, high/low limits their communication to something the other spouse can truly ingest. For the less talkative spouse (in this case, Baron, the husband), "it forces me to give an emotional response to my day instead of simply saying, 'It was fine, same as yesterday.'"

Empathy goes a long way when you're talking during travel separation. Cristina shows her sensitivity when she admits:

> Baron isn't always in a talking mood, and life in the military is such that he may not have much to say, even if he's been out in the field for a week and just got back to base. It's exhausting out in the field, and I had to learn how not to take it personally, as if he isn't interested in me and the kids, and instead realize it'll be a great conversation when he's back in that mindset. I can't force it. It doesn't mean he doesn't love me; it means he's had a really tough week, and he's exhausted and needs time to recover.

I always appreciated Lisa's empathy when I'd call her on Saturday evening after a full Friday/Saturday church conference, knowing I was still going to preach several services on Sunday morning. She could tell from the tone of my voice on Saturday night that there wasn't much left in the tank, and she'd share the most important updates but then say, "I can tell you need to rest. I'll be praying for you." Many times, it's not that you don't care; it's that you lack the energy to show it. The empathy my wife showed in keeping the conversation short made me feel more loved than any attempt she might have made to have a long-drawn-out discussion just to "put in our time."

That doesn't mean the traveling spouse shouldn't make an effort, of course. If you know you can't handle a thirty-minute conversation, give your spouse the best ten-minute conversation you can. A friend I'll call Margo has a husband who likes to connect on the phone throughout the day. Margo has a demanding job that requires a lot of attention and many decisions, but she and her husband have learned that if she says, "Babe, I'm all yours for three minutes, but I've got a firm three o'clock that I have to hang up for," her husband doesn't take it personally. Margo listens attentively and responds directly, and her husband feels welcomed rather than ignored. Since he's an extrovert, he just wants his wife to know what he's thinking about as much as he wants her counsel, so sometimes a simple "We can talk more about this tonight" suffices.

Cristina has a friend whose husband flies commercial airplanes. They spend a lot of time apart, and her friend can tell when her husband isn't engaged when they talk. "He might be on the phone, but his eyes are on Facebook or the television." FaceTime can help with that, forcing you to listen with your eyes as much as your ears. Remove the distractions and think of the conversation as a sprint—you'll give your best as long as you can—rather than a marathon, sauntering along with only partial attention. When you're done, you're done, but be fully present until you hit that spot.

Cristina puts it this way: "Let your wife know she is your only focus. Emails can wait. You can turn on the television in a few moments. While you're talking to her, give her everything you have left."

On other occasions, the traveling spouse may not be tempted by weariness but rather by adrenaline and excitement. Baron spoke of a recruiting trip he took with two other chaplains. They were hanging out every night as "brothers in arms," which distracted him and kept him from talking to Cristina as often as he usually did when he was by himself. She was understandably bothered by this. "Hey, you're out there having fun and don't have any time for us?" Never forget, you're still a spouse even when you're not *with* your spouse. At home, you'd never go out three or four nights in a row without taking your spouse into consideration; don't do that on the road either. Make some time.

Cristina is a big advocate of talking about the trip before you leave. "It really helps when Baron tells me, 'I'm going to be out in the field from this date to this date, but I should be back on base on this particular date.'" For business travel, explain to your husband or wife, "The conference runs late on Thursday and I have an early Friday meeting, but I should be able to touch base in the afternoon." Let them know that a missed evening phone call is about your schedule, not your lack of interest.

Before they deploy, Baron urges couples to utilize the regular postcard practice and use the high/low conversational tool. "I don't want them to just grit their teeth and wait until they're back together. It's not easy to stay connected when you're apart, but if you don't work on staying connected while you're apart, you're training yourselves to live without each other, and that can lead to marital separation."

I'd add that our marriage vows don't include time-outs for vocational separations. Just because it's not as easy to stay connected doesn't mean we're excused from trying. It's not ideal to live apart from each other, even for short periods of time, but it's our job to make the separations as good as possible, given the circumstances and limitations.

THE GOD FACTOR

Christians who travel have a decided advantage. The Holy Spirit binds us even when our bodies are far apart. God's love can bring us together, even when his will is for us to temporarily live apart.

I'm not speaking just metaphorically here. I realize some may think this idea is getting too mystical, but the apostle Paul dared to push this reality of believers being present even when apart to the fullest extent when he told the Colossians, "Though I am absent from you in body, I am present with you in spirit" (Colossians 2:5). He also told the Corinthians, "Even though I am not physically present, I am with you in spirit" (1 Corinthians 5:3). This idea of being "together in spirit" is a pattern with Paul, a foundational understanding of what life in Christ entails. Forced separation can help us learn this truth—one that couples who are always together may never experience.

I realize this kind of language may make some people uncomfortable, but Christianity *is* a supernatural faith. If we are in Christ, the Holy Spirit is a real presence in our lives, and the same Holy Spirit within each of us can help join us even when we are apart. Renowned New Testament scholar Dr. Gordon Fee explains Paul's words to the Corinthians in this way:

> Paul does not mean that in some vague way they are to think about him as though he were actually among them, but is not really so. Rather, when the Corinthians are assembled, the Spirit is understood to be present among them . . . and for Paul that means that he, too, is present among them by that same Spirit. If all of that is not easy for us to grasp, we must nonetheless not try to make Paul think or talk like us.[13]

Seeking to grasp the impact of Paul's linguistics, Fee comes to a surprising conclusion: "Paul does not say . . . 'when you are assembled and I am with you in spirit.' He says, 'when you and my spirit are assembled.'"[14]

We may not be able to grasp, let alone experience, the full reality Paul is addressing here, but it is certainly more than a simple "You are in my thoughts and prayers." A much deeper connection and much more intimate joining are intended.

Perhaps Paul is pointing toward something that podcasters Joanna and Rob Teigen experienced during the years when Rob frequently traveled for business. "One thing that is of great comfort to me," says Joanna, "is that Rob and I have the same Spirit of God because we are both followers of Jesus, so even if Rob is across an ocean, we can still be unified in the Spirit. It has been amazing how God may put the same burden on both of our hearts at the same time . . . That was always reassuring to me."[15]

Which means if you want to make your marriage a fortress against marital separations, a major step for both spouses is to draw ever closer to God while they are apart. Surrender to the presence of God's Spirit and be united in your mutual faith in Christ.

WHAT ABOUT SEX?

As a chaplain, Baron is completely comfortable talking about the most intimate aspects of marital separation, including a realistic but God-honoring approach to handling sex and temptation during long absences. When I asked him how he became so comfortable with this, he laughed and explained how his mom informed him that the beanbag chair that sat in his room when he was a teenager was the exact piece of furniture on which he had been conceived. And then she added that the reason his middle name is "Clint" is because a Clint Eastwood movie was playing *while* he was conceived. If Baron can have a conversation like that with his mother, talking to fellow soldiers and their spouses is easy.

The "intensity" of Baron's return depends on how long he has been away. If he's coming home from a three-day trip, he sends his kids on a thirty-minute walk down the street with the dog, just to reset his mind. When he comes back from trips that last months, "I don't have the bandwidth to deal with a wife and kids together. To be honest, I usually have one thing on my mind, and that's sex."

Especially for younger husbands, Baron and Cristina's model of separating his reunion with the wife and kids is a great idea. "The first time we did this, Cristina picked me up by herself, and we went to a hotel for one night and came home late the next day. It was wonderful, the 'first time' everything in eight months—the first steak dinner, first night out with my wife, first time to have sex, all that."

It worked out so well that after the next deployment, Cristina picked him up and they spent two nights and two days together, going to a comedy show, staying in a nice hotel, eating great food. "We tend to be frugal, but we spare no expense for the reunion."

I love this model. I wish Lisa and I had been more thoughtful about this when I traveled so much while the kids were young. The opportunity to be intimate and become a couple again freed Baron and Christina to be more focused parents when they returned to their kids. It's a bit more sensible than trying to put them to bed at 5:00 p.m. just so you and your spouse can have some "alone time"!

Sadly, Baron doesn't see many military couples follow this pattern. "The typical excuse is that they don't have anybody to watch the kids. Well, you've got six months to find somebody. You're in the military. You can figure it out. That's what we do—solve dangerous problems."

He points out, "If we're not connected as a couple, we don't function as well as parents, so it's much better to reconnect and then join together as parents again."

Cristina values the private reunion because "the spouse who stays home can feel slighted because the kids require so much attention when Daddy gets home. They're all over him, and you have to wait until they go to bed to get your husband all to yourself. And because the returning spouse was trying to emotionally connect with everybody, he might already be tired out by the time you're alone."

To help Baron deal with sexual temptation, his pastor implements what Baron calls the "hotel protocol." Baron lets him know he'll be on the road, and his pastor will send him a text asking how the previous night went. Baron also uses the Covenant Eyes accountability software. Some wives have told him they don't want to micromanage their husbands, saying something like, "That's his own private part of his life," to which Baron responds, "I say that's part of the problem. Married individuals shouldn't have private parts of their life related to sex. If you can't have a real, open, and honest conversation about sexual desires, you're in a distant marriage." (Let me add that many counselors have told me they usually counsel wives *not* to be the accountability partner on software programs; women suffering from betrayal trauma could be triggered and find monitoring to be detrimental to their own healing. In such cases, it's enough to know a brother in the Lord is asking their husbands the tough questions.)

Talking about temptation before a spouse leaves helps a couple prepare for the separation. Baron knows of couples who regularly send erotic photos or who have even filmed "episodes" of themselves together that they'll watch when they're apart. Not every couple will feel comfortable doing this (Lisa and I didn't). You shouldn't expect your spouse to be willing to do this if they aren't comfortable with it themselves; intimacy is built on safety, and if any activity makes a spouse feel less than safe for any reason, it undercuts your marriage rather than serves it.

It's not easy to have conversations like this, but it's much healthier than pretending that temptation on the road or for the one left at home isn't an issue. It usually is. If you talk about it beforehand, you can prepare together rather than leaving one spouse to be strong on their own. Learn how to face temptation *as a couple*, and your marriage will be the stronger for it.

In Dr. Joy Skarka's doctoral dissertation on women and sexual shame, she found that healthy marriages have a healing power to address the sexual shame so many women have felt.[16] Marriage proved healing for the past and helpful for future temptations *if* the women's confessions were met by their husbands with three things: empathy, active listening, and a "we're in this together" attitude, that is, not leaving wives to face their struggle against temptation on their own. Dr. Skarka told me the same is true for husbands.

When a husband or wife feels like they're alone in this struggle, it simply creates additional loneliness that fuels future acting out. And more than a few women—for example, those who struggle with pornography—are silent because they think women aren't supposed to deal with this kind of temptation, and the shame they feel may thus be even greater.

You don't have to spend time apart to learn how to bear each other's burdens. (This advice isn't for those married to addicts. Addicts need professional help that a spouse on their own can't provide. And this isn't meant to make a spouse married to an addict feel like it's their fault if a spouse falls. I talk more about this in chapter 8.) It's particularly important for couples who travel, but sexual temptation is by no means limited to couples who sleep miles apart for days at a time!

Cristina has found that preparing for time away can create an intimacy all its own. "You have to be very comfortable with each other to have these conversations. It takes you out of your comfort zone, but sharing your vulnerabilities draws you closer together. It requires trust that you're not going to be exploited, and of course we tell every couple to double-check and then triple-check to make sure that if you're sending something a little racy, you're sending it to the right person."

This advice comes from experience. One couple Baron worked with accidentally uploaded a bunch of photos to a family platform. Fortunately, the husband immediately noticed it and took everything down before anyone saw it. Apps are now available that give an increased level of privacy for married couples to share intimate things, but please keep in mind that I've also had counselors warn of the danger of anything being out there that could be copied or exploited, not to mention what might happen if (I hate to even mention it, but it's always possible) the marriage were to break up. Couples need to think about this carefully and with counsel.

As a chaplain, Baron has talked to couples who have written out sexual fantasies to each other. The husband might leave something new for the wife to try on while he can be "with her" on FaceTime. But Baron also reminds the traveling spouse that "if your wife is at home with your kids, she doesn't have time to sext you all day. She's not just your wife; she's your kids' mom who has her own job to tend to, so you have to be understanding."

If couples wonder what's okay, Baron's guidance is simple: "If your wife can't or doesn't know about anything you're doing, you shouldn't be doing it." In my opinion, that's wise. Sexual experience in marriage is always meant to be shared. Scripture offers great freedom for married couples with very few restrictions when they act *as a couple*.* Talking about how to navigate separation, fight temptation, and keep the sexual chemistry alive, appropriately so, as you're apart, can build a lot of intimacy.

Baron notes that some creative scheduling may be required. "On one deployment, my morning was Cristina's night, but when you plan ahead and Cristina has the kids asleep and her door locked, you can do all kinds of creative things."

Facing this challenge *together* has been very healthy for Cristina. "I grew up in the church, and the narrative about sex from birth till marriage is danger, danger, danger. And then it seems like we don't help couples once they are married to express the full freedom God gives to us."

Learning how to manage sexual desire—whether you're apart or always together—can do wonders for married couples because it builds honesty, vulnerability, creativity, generosity, and understanding. This is how you strengthen your connection even when you are miles apart.

REENTRY

Baron warns, "If couples aren't thoughtful about staying together when they're apart, they won't know how to be married in physical proximity to each other when they return. They'll just keep growing apart, even when they're back in the same house."

---

* Debra Fileta and I explore this in much more detail in our book *Married Sex: A Christian Couple's Guide to Reimagining Your Love Life* (Grand Rapids: Zondervan, 2021).

Cristina adds, "Even if you stay connected while you're apart, it takes an adjustment when the spouse comes back. You have your own schedule, and you need to be willing to move things around now that your spouse is home."

Baron warns that "many guys find deployment way easier than coming home. Some of them have even told me they'd rather go back to war!"

Small things like sending flowers to your spouse when you're away, each of you expressing empathy for the challenges the other one is facing, making time for focused phone calls, and keeping some form of sexual intimacy alive will help keep you growing together. A military spouse asked us to send copies of *Devotions for a Sacred Marriage* to their respective addresses so that they could read through the devotions and spend a few minutes talking about them together on the phone.[17] Putting your marriage on hold, thinking you can just pick it up again later, rarely works.

"Vocational separation just compresses what you often see," says Baron, "when a couple is married for twenty-five years and is just waiting for the kids to leave for college until they get divorced."

I love Baron's take on this. If we foster selfishness for any period of time, acting like we're not married and not parents, we won't suddenly become "unselfish" when we get back together. *Choices carve character.* It's unwise to try to "ride out" separations, because even if you decide to turn back when you return, you've already ridden a long way in opposite directions, and the relationship will feel distant accordingly. We are just as married on the road as we are at home, and we need to act like it if we want our marriage to remain a fortress.

Cristina warns, "If you're disconnected from your spouse the whole time they're gone, you start to think, *Hey, I can do this.* And in some ways, there may be fewer interruptions and fewer annoyances. You don't have to *imagine* life without your spouse; you're living it! Which means divorce doesn't sound so scary. You feel like you've already learned how to manage being separated."

We can mentally divorce our spouse before we legally divorce our spouse if we're not careful.

COUNT THE COST

Though Baron and Cristina have learned to thrive while being apart from each other, they admit that accepting a life of vocational separation isn't for everyone.

"I'm a wanderlust, adventure-seeking guy," Baron admits. "I *like* the moving and the travel and even getting into sticky situations around the world. It took a little longer for Cristina to be able to accept me doing that. I *don't* think every couple is called to a lifestyle where separation is a regular part of their relationship."

Cristina concurs. "It's not just about the spouse who travels. It also requires something special for the person who stays home. You have to be able to live without regular communication for a while. You have to be able to handle days where everything falls apart and there's no one to turn to but yourself. You have to be the kind of person who can make decisions without your spouse and not resent it."

At first, Baron and Cristina didn't know how Cristina would handle their separations, but they got a quick introduction when Baron went to Afghanistan. The first day he was gone, Cristina's car got a flat tire *and* she found out their son needed his tonsils and adenoids removed. If having to go through that alone seems like too much to handle, it's probably best for your spouse to find a job that keeps them at home. While many couples have been able to grow together and keep their marriage strong in the face of frequent separations, it's better to admit that, for whatever reason, you can't or don't want to be apart rather than risk sacrificing your marriage for the sake of your job.

On the *Growing Home Together* podcast, Joanna and Rob shared that they reached their limit one time after Joanna dropped Rob off at the airport and as they said goodbye, their kids didn't cry. That made Joanna break into tears later that night as she shared her heart with their small group. "They just acted like it's normal for a daddy to be gone. It should *not* feel normal for my husband and my kids' dad to be away."[18]

Not long after that, Rob started making decisions about his career and how often he wanted to be away. He eventually moved into a position that required much less travel.

While Baron enjoys the adventure-seeking life, he is sensitive to Cristina's limit. "When we decided to do this Navy thing, I told Cristina she has 100 percent veto power over every tour I take. If one comes up and she just can't handle it, I'll pull the plug on the whole military career. My marriage is more important than my job. While I'm right where I believe God wants me to be, I don't believe he calls us to just one thing. There are a lot of ways I can practice my faith and Christian leadership other than being in the Marine Corps. I'm married to Cristina; I'm not married to the title, rank, and bling on my chest."

And with that attitude, Baron and Cristina have made their marriage a fortress that actually grows stronger though separation instead of weaker.

You have been my refuge,

a strong tower against the foe. (Psalm 61:3)

Building Your Fortress Takeaways

1. If you must spend time apart, it's essential that you not put your marriage on hold. Keep growing closer together even while spending time apart.

2. Choices carve character.

3. Both spouses need to be honest and explicit about their expectations for what will happen while they're apart, and what will happen when they reconnect. Your expectations will exist whether you verbalize them or not, so it's best to discuss them together.

4. Expectations are acceptable requests, but they can't be demands. Just because we'd prefer something to be different doesn't mean it's realistic for our spouse to do that.

5. A technique like "high/low" can foster the most productive conversations if your brain is fatigued at the end of a long day.

6. Have empathy for each other. Exhaustion and loneliness make life difficult; don't fault your spouse for being drained by life. Try to build them up.

7. If you can't handle a long conversation, give your spouse the best ten-minute conversation you can. Be fully present for as long as you're engaged with each other.

8. Marriage vows don't include time-outs for vocational separations. Just because it's not as easy to stay connected doesn't mean you're excused from trying. If you don't try to stay close while you're apart, you're training yourselves to live without each other, and that can lead to marital separation.

9. Christians who travel have the added benefit of unity in the Holy Spirit.

10. If the separation has been a long one, it can be beneficial for the husband and wife to get together before reconnecting with the kids.

11. Talking about how to handle sexual temptation as a couple, even though you'll be apart, can build a lot of intimacy, trust, and gratitude and lead to increased feelings of attachment and togetherness.

12. Don't try to simply ride out or endure separations; instead, find ways to stay connected, or else the reunion will feel distant and awkward. We can mentally divorce our spouse before we legally divorce our spouse if we're not careful.

13. Count the cost of frequent or long-term separations before you accept such a lifestyle. Some couples decide their relationship can't handle it, or they simply prefer not to choose it.

CHAPTER 4

EMOTIONAL ATTACHMENT AFTER BETRAYAL

The Three Foundational Building Blocks of a Marital Fortress

D r. Archibald Hart and Dr. Sharon May are adherents of what is called "attachment theory," where the most important thing to focus on in marriage is *emotional connection*. Emotional connection is what keeps your marriage strong even when everything seems to be ripping the two of you apart.

Throughout my life I've focused on spiritual connection first and foremost, beginning with our connection to God, but maybe that's because I'm a teacher and pastor, not a psychologist (as Dr. Hart was and Dr. May is). But whether or not emotional connection is the primary need, it is certainly an essential component of an intimate marriage—in some ways, it's the very definition of an intimate marriage.

Hart and May point out, "The building blocks that our clinical experience and research have shown to be essential to a safe haven marriage are trust, emotional availability, and sensitive responsiveness."[19] If there has been a *distractedness* that keeps us from being available to each other, *apathy* that cultivates callous insensitivity, and then a *betrayal* that breaks trust, the marriage is going to be severely threatened, if not destroyed. However, these same three elements—trust, emotional availability, and sensitive responsiveness—can be the building blocks to put a distant marriage back together and rebuild it into a fortress.[20]

Emotional availability means you create the space to demonstrate and express concern for your spouse's hurts, fears, hopes, and joys. You don't try to solve their problems so much as you sit with them in their problems, hear their frustrations, and share in their triumphs. You make mental space for them—that's what it means to be "available." It might best be described with three powerful relationship-building words: "Tell me more." Whatever they are feeling is more important than what you are doing.

Sensitive responsiveness is a learned skill. You don't respond with immediate judgment or ridicule. You don't try to dismiss the issue just to get over it; you hear them out and walk with them through the process of their expression. Make sure you *respond*, and make sure you're *sensitive*. Base your posture on your answers to these questions: How can I make this conversation feel safe for my spouse as it begins? How can I make them feel heard and understood as it ends?

Trust is a by-product. If you said you'd pick up milk at the grocery store and didn't, you broke trust, which will have a relational consequence. For your spouse to feel intimately connected with you, they need to know they can depend on you and that you will tell them the truth. If you lie once, how will they know you're ever telling the truth? To feel closer to your spouse and to help your spouse feel closer to you, do what you say you'll do and be someone your spouse can count on. On the flip side, if your spouse has earned your trust, make sure you give it. Suspicion is the enemy of intimacy. It needs to be pointed out that the foundation of trust is safety. Hart and May are adamant about this: "Marriages are never safe havens when there is physical or emotional abuse."[21]

What I like about naming these three elements is that they help us see what we need to keep a marriage strong or to put a marriage back together. In this chapter, we're going to meet a couple who typify how a lack of trust, emotional availability, and sensitive responsiveness can turn a white-hot romance into an arctic winter, but we'll also look at how regaining all three (in some very creative ways) can rebuild a broken marriage.

DYNAMITE

Betrayal is to marriage what dynamite is to a door—it blows everything apart. The betrayal can be sharing a private confidence. It can be an emotional affair. It can be looking at something on the internet that grieves your spouse. It can be taking family money and using it to feed a gambling addiction or to make a large purchase you haven't agreed on. It can be belittling your spouse behind their back. It can be indulging an addiction (drug or alcohol abuse) after you had promised to stop. In all these situations, it's not just what you did; it's *who* you betrayed. Individuals sometimes focus on the deed that was *done* rather than on the relational betrayal that was *felt*.

At first, the betrayed spouse asks, "How could you do that?"

And then they naturally make it personal: "How could you do that *to me*?" How, indeed, can you share further intimacies with someone you no longer trust? How can you share your heart and your future with someone who has betrayed you?

Betrayal doesn't *have* to end a marriage, however. Reconciliation will require much repentance and much forgiveness, but if both parties are willing to walk a difficult path, they can find themselves in an even deeper relationship than the one they knew before the betrayal took place. Repentance is essential, however. The betrayal must stop before reconnection can even be contemplated, much less pursued.

Terri and David aren't just living embodiments of how attachment theory can renew a marriage; they are also models of how long it can take to begin walking in newness of life. Any kind of betrayal will require more than one talk and one act of forgiveness. What we'll see in their story is what can be true of yours. Throughout this long process, God, the author and finisher of our faith, is working to bring us back together, even as our own actions threaten to tear us apart.

FALLING IN LUST

Many couples have told me how they "fell in love." Terri is the first one who told me she and David got married right out of college because they "fell in lust."

They weren't believers at the time and gave birth to two babies in pretty quick succession.

Caring for a toddler and a baby at the same time will often make lust feel like a distant memory instead of a current companion, and that's exactly what happened to David and Terri. From once just wanting to tear each other's clothes off, they found themselves wanting to tear each other's eyes out.

David responded to the emotional disconnect by looking elsewhere to meet his emotional needs. With the added mouths to feed, he knew they needed more money and a bigger house, so he landed a consulting job in Houston, rose quickly up the ranks, and started getting requests to travel throughout Texas.

Money started pouring in. David and Terri bought a new house and a new car, and his company started sending David to engagements all across the United States. For three years, he left the house on Sunday and came back on Friday.

"We didn't have a strong enough foundation in our marriage to survive that," Terri admits. "David came home, and we'd fight. He would say, 'I'm so tired from traveling. I need to rest,' and I'd say, 'Are you kidding me? I'm taking care of the house, raising two little kids while also working a full-time job, *and* I take care of all the finances, and you think *you're* the one who needs a rest?'"

They weren't emotionally available to each other, and neither was responding sensitively to the other. On the contrary, they did the exact opposite. They fought all weekend. Terri says, "He'd leave on Sunday night with us screaming at each other and hating each other. We both wanted a divorce, but neither of us had the courage to call a lawyer."

Today, Terri and David adore each other. Terri recently told me that the twenty-ninth year of their marriage has been the *best* year of their marriage. I point this out to stress that a couple can all but hate each other one year and then, through growth, change and faith, learn to cherish and delight in each other. It has happened to others, and it can happen to you.

THE AFFAIR

In the midst of her deep and pervasive disappointment, Terri eventually sought comfort in the arms of a coworker. "My coworker started out by flirting with me and giving me compliments. To be honest, I never felt an emotional connection with him. It just felt good because he was giving me what David wasn't. And then it turned physical. It wasn't because of some overpowering sexual allure. It was more that here was someone who wanted me when my husband didn't." Terri said that her greatest need was "knowing I was worthy of being pursued," a need that wasn't being met at home.

Terri's wading into an affair is rather common. Affairs aren't always about falling in love, which typically would set off alarms in your brain. They're often not even about lust, which we're more spiritually attuned to and may guard against. In Terri's case, the slow descent to having an affair began by living with an obvious, unfulfilled desire to be wanted, which set her up to be wooed, which set her up to start seeking out her coworker just to talk to him, which set her up to receive his flirtations when he started giving them, which set her up to allow him to kiss her at a bar one evening, which set her up to meet him for their first full sexual encounter. Affairs are frequently *gradual*, entered into by many little steps. In time, little steps can carry us a long way, which is why we want to be careful about taking the first step in the wrong direction.

If you get anything out of this chapter, please get this: little betrayals are stepping-stones to big betrayals. Consider every *little* step away from your spouse as a major assault on your union. Lying and hiding to any degree open the door to things much worse than what you're initially lying about and hiding.

Toward the end of the three-month affair, Terri and David went to see a Sandra Bullock movie, *Hope Floats*, whose plot centers around a marital affair. "Terri would pull away from me during the movie," David recalls. "She wouldn't let me hold her hand or put my arm around her. I tried to talk to her about it to find out what was going on, but that's the night it all blew up."

Feeling Terri's lack of affection (emotional availability) and frustrated by her refusal to talk about it (sensitive responsiveness), David blew up and said, "I'm done. I'm *done*."

Terri remembers, "I could tell from the look on his face that he meant it. The really sad thing is that at first I was actually relieved. I yelled back, 'Good! I hate you! I'm glad it's done!'"

Terri didn't have a personal relationship with the Lord, but she had gone to church for much of her life and suddenly felt God getting hold of her. She started shaking and cried out, "David, don't go, please. Don't go. We can make this marriage work. We can start over again."

David left anyway and drove to a hotel, but after he checked into his room, he realized he couldn't just give up on his marriage. He *wasn't* done. He came back home and found Terri flooding their bed with her tears.

They talked and even prayed. Terri believes that was the night she entered into a real relationship with God. I love how the difficulties of marriage can point us to a new dependence on God.

In an earnest attempt to rekindle their family's togetherness, they planned a weekend camping trip, which went wonderfully. The last morning they were there, Terri went down to the lake to have a "beautiful quiet time with the Lord."

Terri relates that when she walked back to the campground, "David came out of the tent with a solemn look on his face. He was almost glowing. He told me, 'I just had this strangest dream about honesty, integrity, and truth. I looked down at the blanket and saw a picture of Jesus.'"

Terri started shaking, and soon she couldn't breathe.

"Terri, what is it?"

"David, I know why you had that dream. I wasn't going to tell you this, but God is telling me now that I have to tell you something. The last three months while you were traveling, I had an affair with a man at work. I just ended it. God revealed to me that you weren't fulfilling every need and desire, that I was putting way too many expectations on you, expectations you couldn't possibly fill. So I went to find someone who could. But God showed me this morning that he's the only one who can fill that void in my heart. David, I am so sorry, and I release you from all the expectations I have put on you. God tells me in his Word that he forgives me, but it's going to take me a long time to forgive myself. I'm praying that you can find it in your heart to forgive me too."

David's response wasn't what Terri had hoped. "When Terri confessed her affair," David says, "my world came crashing down. Everything I put my trust in—my work, the money, my family, a faithful wife—all those pillars came crashing down, and I went into a rage."

David packed up the entire camp in about ten minutes, made Terri sit in the back seat, and drove "about 110 miles an hour" down I-10.

When they stopped for gas, David got out to "call our friends, my mother, Terri's parents, our marriage counselor—everybody I could think of—to tell them, 'This is why we're getting a divorce. It's all been a mirage.'"

Hours later, as David pulled into their driveway in Houston, "standing on my front porch was the very last person I ever wanted to see—my father."

David's father left his family when David was twelve and immediately married his secretary. David had barely talked to him in seven years, but his mom had called him to say, "You need to get over to David's house."

David got out of his car and ran up the stairs to his home office to comb through files of credit card statements, phone records, emails—any evidence he could find. It was all there. "Like a big jigsaw puzzle, everything fit together, and I felt so stupid for missing all the signals. I was trying to figure out why. Was it about all my traveling? Of course, I didn't consider that I might have had something to do with it."

David's father followed David around the house, urging him to calm down. "You're too emotional. You don't need to make any decisions right now."

"Oh yeah? Well, I'm making one." Turning to Terri, he said, "Terri, you have one hour to get out of the house. And by the way, the kids are mine."

David's dad managed to get David and Terri into an empty room. After David spent an hour expressing his hurt—"How could you do this to me? What about our family, our children? What will the neighbors think?"—he came out of the room and got the most surprising invitation of his life.

"David, I'd like you to come to church with me."

During the seven years of their separation, David's dad had become a Christian, and he was now inviting David to go with him to church.

"Dad, that's not going to happen. I don't own a Bible. I don't know God, and if there is a God, I'm pretty sure he doesn't know me." But David was in such a state of confusion and helplessness that he finally agreed to go, and so the next morning he found himself sitting at one end of the pew with Terri at the other and their kids in between.

"Everything the pastor said was like salve to a deep wound. I felt like I was the only one in the sanctuary. How did he know? I kept saying to myself, *Give me more!* I couldn't get enough."

God used more than David's father to turn his attention toward Jesus. He also used David's father-in-law. As soon as Terri's dad got David's angry phone message about what Terri had done, he jumped on a red-eye flight to Houston and walked into their house at 2:00 a.m. holding a Bible.

"I want you to have this, and even more, I want us to study this together. You can ask me any question you want about it."

David wasn't sure where to start. He figured that since there was an "Old" Testament and a "New" Testament, he might as well begin with the "newer, improved" edition and found himself reading through the genealogy in Matthew. And then he came to the story of Jesus' conception and birth.

"So now I have one question," David asked his father-in-law. "Why did Joseph stay with Mary?"

"What do you mean?"

"Mary had an affair, and the boy is clearly not Joseph's, so why would Joseph want to stay?"

"David, I've never heard it put that way before. Let's talk about who Jesus actually was and is."

Following that conversation, Terri's father (who, as we'll learn later, once had his own marital challenges to overcome) led David to Christ.

Both David and Terri became spiritually hungry. "For two years, every time the church doors were open, we were there."

Their marriage, however, was still in shambles. Spiritual rehabilitation doesn't make marital rehabilitation automatic. You still have to rebuild trust, emotional availability, and sensitive responsiveness. A horrific crash ultimately became the catalyst for David and Terri to get past the betrayal and learn how to reconnect emotionally.

THE CRASH

"For two years we wore a mask; I could never bring myself to forgive Terri for the affair, nor could I ever bring myself to utter the words, 'I love you.' We were just cohabiting, planning on hanging in there until the kids left for college, and then we'd quit."

Living in the same house doesn't make your marriage a fortress; living in the same shared experience does. You can share a bed and be miles apart as you sleep. You can sleep miles apart and be intimately connected, as long as you share trust, emotional availability, and sensitive responsiveness to each other's needs. Emotional distance is a much greater threat than physical distance.

David and Terri agreed to chaperone a youth trip to Colorado. On the return trip, the bus driver was furious with the group for delaying his departure by many hours, making him fearful he'd miss his driver connection. He drove recklessly down the mountain on perilously slippery roads, only to lose control and drive the bus over the edge of a cliff. The roof of the bus was entirely ripped off, and sixty-five youth and six adults—including Terri,

David, and their two children—were thrown over the side of the mountain.

Three people died, and almost all the passengers were seriously wounded. Terri was among the worst. She suffered a shattered hip, a spine broken in several places, multiple broken ribs, and serious head wounds.

David woke up with two broken arms, broken ribs, torn ligaments, and a particularly nasty head wound.

Emergency personnel flew all the casualties to five different hospitals. By some miracle, David and his children were sent to the same one. When David regained consciousness and asked about Terri, nobody had a clue where she was.

"In that moment of uncertainty I began to pray out loud," says David. "God, why did you allow this to happen? It doesn't make sense."

Almost immediately, David heard in his mind, *You're done. David, you're done—with your career, your money, your toys, your selfishness, your bitterness, your unforgiveness. You're done. You need to find Terri and tell her you forgive her and love her.*

Isn't this just like God? We go to him filled with anger and bitterness about what our spouse has done. God comes back to us and sometimes puts the onus on us—what *we* have done and what *we* need to change. It can be hard to receive that conviction when everyone would agree with David that what Terri had done was wrong, grievously so. But for them to reconnect, it was necessary for David to surrender to God's spiritual soul-searching.

Two days went by before David was wheeled into Terri's room, but when he finally was, he thought there must have been a mistake. The woman lying in the bed couldn't be Terri. Her head was bloated to the size of a basketball, to the point where he didn't recognize her. When the nurses assured him that the woman lying there was his wife, David asked everybody to leave the room.

Alone with his unconscious wife, David leaned down and spoke into Terri's ear. "Terri, I don't know if you can hear me, but I need you to know that I totally forgive you for the affair, and I am so in love with you."

Four months and multiple surgeries later, Terri was finally able to leave the hospital, but she came home to a very different husband.

At the time, David was an executive at Hewlett Packard. After he got back from his own recovery, a vice president offered him any position he wanted. "If you want Asia, it's yours. If you want Europe, it's yours. Just name it."

David sighed and said, "Don, I'm done."

"What?"

"I'm done. I believe in my heart that God has called me into full-time vocational ministry."

They sold everything—the six-thousand-square-foot home that sat on a golf course, their cars, most of their possessions—and offered themselves up to become totally available for the Lord.

WHAT WENT WRONG?

Terri shares the reason she believes she was particularly vulnerable to an affair:

I had baggage from my own childhood and past, including huge insecurities I didn't understand how much had affected me. I always had to have a boyfriend and be wanted. Because I didn't have a relationship with Christ, I was seeking affirmation from other people. David and I jumped into marriage with immaturity and no spiritual foundation. It was just, "Let's get married." We didn't talk about our past, our expectations, and didn't get any counseling at all. We weren't prepared. It was all about lust. Once the lust died, there was nothing holding us together.

Looking back, we had grossly unrealistic expectations of a "happily ever after" kind of life. Part of what helped heal us, to be honest, was reading *Sacred Marriage*. When you wrote about marriage being designed for our holiness even more than our happiness, we started to get an entirely new mindset that could affair-proof our marriage.

In addition to coming into marriage with a lot of baggage and misguided expectations, Terri believes a third element that led to the affair was "not prioritizing our marriage. If couples aren't intentional about investing in each other, they become prideful and self-consumed. I was consumed with my job and raising the kids, and David was consumed with his job. We didn't prioritize our marriage at all, nor did we put any work toward it. We just expected it to stay strong and grow on its own. That doesn't work."

David concurs. "We responded to our deep emptiness by gravitating to our own personal refuges where our emotional needs could be met. For both of us, that was work. Terri's coworker [the one she had an affair with] was telling her everything she wanted to hear—'It must be hard for you; you deserve so much more than what you're getting'—that he was essentially promoting her sense of self-entitlement. That created a chasm of disconnect so that when we did see each other, we usually just fought. We were coping at best rather than relating on an intimate level."

Drs. Hart and May warn:

Emotional disconnection doesn't require an emotional earthquake. Just pile on the critical comments, insensitive remarks, and irritating acts, whether intentional or unintentional, and you can break your partner's heart. Not much more than a flat-toned hello from your spouse after you've waited all day to see him, a kiss that did not seem warm, a hand touched then quickly pulled away, unwillingness to stop for a hug, failure to help get the kids up and ready in time for school, the thoughtlessness of not putting the dirty dishes in the sink, clothes left in the hallway, or not having time to listen when a listening ear is desperately needed—all these can do deep damage, one bit at a time.[22]

When you know there is distance in your marriage, you have two options: cope with the pain by "spiritually medicating" it (with workaholism, excessive gaming, affairs, and so forth), or remove the cause of the pain—namely, the distance between the two of you. In their marriage seminars, Terri and David stress the need to build the "five layers of intimacy": spiritual, sexual, sensual, emotional, and intellectual.* Having worked with so many couples who have had affairs, David and Terri note that sexual intimacy is often the easiest to maintain:

---

* David and Terri founded Marriage Life Ministries, which has a special focus on adventure-based therapy. (www.marriagelifeministries.com). They lead workshops and retreats all over the country.

So many couples admit there's absolutely zero spiritual, emotional, intellectual, or sensual intimacy, but the sex is off the charts. But it's a different *kind* of sex. It's not sensual; it's athletic. There's no passionate kissing in the sense of connecting, no looking into each other's eyes or enjoying each other's presence. It's more using each other's bodies to get sexual release.

Which means that just because a couple is still having sex doesn't mean everything is okay. Pay attention to the *kind* of sex you're having. Is it about connecting, giving to each other, enjoying each other, or is it about using each other to meet your physical needs? Sexuality divorced from sensuality is a serious red flag. If you're great at intercourse but reluctant to kiss passionately and look each other in the eye, there may be a serious problem. It's hard to betray your spouse on any level and look them in the eye, even when you're having sex.

Terri and David remember that they still (occasionally) had sex even during Terri's affair, "but there was a noticeable emotional and sensual difference. When we did have intercourse, it was just going through the motions."

That changed dramatically soon after the affair was confessed. "David had a business trip in Boston and insisted I go with him because he didn't trust me. We had the most amazing, passionate sex we had ever had up until then, and we reached a level of intimacy we had never known before."

So if you're wondering if an affair or broken trust means a marriage must end, or if regaining intimacy is impossible, you should know it's possible to experience a *deeper* level of intimacy and satisfaction after the affair than what you had before the affair.

EMOTIONAL ATTACHMENT AFTER BETRAYAL

If your partner is repentant and ruthlessly pursues honesty, emotional attachment may be just around the corner. Of course, to regain intimacy, you will need to assume they are no longer lying about how they're managing their finances, acting out on the internet, or becoming emotionally involved with anyone else. You can't reconnect with your spouse if you haven't first disconnected from whatever caused the broken trust.

David explains:

> The sex was so good because we reached a level of transparency we had never known before. While trying to process the affair, I had asked Terri a jillion questions: "Where were you when you first kissed?" "What hotel did you go to?"—things like that. And then I'd ask the same questions a dozen different ways hoping to trip her up to get the real answer because I still didn't totally believe her. On the Boston trip, Terri was leaning up on the headboard when I went into my routine, and she finally said, "David, you've asked that question a hundred times already, but I'm an open book, and I will answer it as many times as you need me to."

Notice what Terri did. Her answer typifies emotional availability and sensitive responsiveness. And that opened David's heart. He responded, "'That's what I've wanted you to say all along. I don't need to ask you any more questions.' And that's when the great sex started."

Terri adds, "The reason for that is we finally achieved emotional and relational intimacy. We felt connected to each other, with no putting up our guard at all. That sexual feast provided the kind of emotional high we needed to get through all the pain that was still ahead. David still had not fully forgiven me, and there were many dark days in front of us."

WHAT MAKES US VULNERABLE?

David believes that if you want to make your marriage a fortress against sexual temptation, you need to focus on building other kinds of intimacy. "Transparency in all aspects is crucial. Make sure you have open lines of communication and that you freely talk about your wants, desires, and needs, especially the emotional and spiritual but the sexual as well."

He notes that husbands in particular often shut down when talking about their sexual desires because they feel shamed or humiliated and decide to go it alone. That makes a man particularly vulnerable to straying. It doesn't ever excuse him for straying, but it does make him a prime candidate. David says:

> We believe one of a woman's greatest emotional needs is to be valued and pursued. We believe one of a man's greatest emotional needs is to know he has what it takes to be successful, whether in the garage, at the grill, in the boardroom, or even in the bedroom. As guys age, it's increasingly difficult to talk about what's happening to our bodies and how we're going to begin facing challenges we never had as younger men. To say "I'm struggling" is to say I don't have what it takes to be successful in the bedroom, and that's devastating to a man's sense of self-worth.

Terri believes that part of why she was vulnerable to an affair had to do with David's abandonment of the family, having become so focused on providing financially that he paid little attention to their emotional and spiritual support. "And to make things worse," says Terri, "as he traveled he was constantly affirmed and praised, something I never gave him at home, so the road became more pleasant."

Accordingly, David was the first to volunteer to go to the "outposts"—the out-of-the-way business trips that required more travel. His billable hours per week were off the charts as he was occasionally gone for fourteen-day stretches. Every hour he billed at work, of course, was one less hour he spent at home.

"I was succeeding on the road, but every time I came home, all I heard was, 'David, you don't have what it takes to be a husband or spiritual leader.' I wasn't a Christian; I didn't even know what a spiritual leader was!"

As sometimes happens with a spouse in a spiritually unequal marriage, Terri had to learn not to reinforce this notion of David's failure even as she prayed for him. "When Terri and I first started praying," says David, "her prayers sounded like she was trying to fix me. I didn't feel respected or appreciated."

I've heard other spouses give similar accounts, so be warned. It's possible for joint prayer to hurt your marriage if you're not thoughtful about how you pray and what you're praying about. You may be sending a cruel message to your spouse, even as you think you're casting your cares on God. Praying, "God, help Antoine become a better spiritual leader," or "Please give Jade more patience with the kids," may not be received as an encouragement. These kinds of prayers sound like criticism. God can hear you when you're praying on your own just as well as when you're with your spouse, so you may want to keep some of your prayers between you and God.

BUILDING THE FORTRESS

After David quit his job at Hewlett Packard, he and Terri began leading adventure-based marriage retreats. Their belief is that teaching on its own doesn't always produce long-term change, but couples who participate in marital adventure programs are more likely to report having sustained levels of increased marital satisfaction long after the program has ended.[23] David and Terri use a game where the wife is in the middle of a hula hoop while other couples are throwing balls. It's the husband's job to run around and protect his wife. The game mimics real life in that many spouses aren't aware of the balls being hurtled at their spouse: "Bills, stress, kids, sexual temptation, unemployment," say David and Terri, "the reality is that so many balls are flying toward our spouses that if we don't stay connected, we can't protect them. We'll miss them."

How can we better prepare for these "balls"? David and Terri laugh. "Our favorite answer was when a husband suggested, 'Get rid of the person who is throwing the ball!' There's a lot of truth in that. How many unforeseen things are we allowing to come into our marriage that have no business coming at us?"

Which means, practically speaking, that protecting your marriage—making it a fortress—means saying no in advance to possible triggers. David explains, "We live in a different time. We have counseled many couples about infidelity, and about 70 percent of the time, the affair is between a spouse and a CrossFit or gym trainer, especially for wives."

There's an interesting explanation for this. Renowned psychologist and relationship expert Dr. John Gottman has demonstrated that elevated heartbeats (ninety-five beats or more per minute) put our brains in a heightened state of emotion, which leads to a more meaningful conversation during or immediately after the activity, which gives a couple a better chance of creating a positive memory. That's why David and Terri like to use strenuous activities or even scary ones (like high-wire obstacle courses—which also rebuild *trust*) after a time of teaching. The elevated heart rate creates a new vulnerability, which can foster a new connection.

For married couples, an understanding of the vulnerability resulting from an elevated heartbeat can be sacred. Outside of marriage, that dynamic can become the portal to betrayal. What gets your heartbeat above ninety-five beats per minute? CrossFit and running groups, to name just a couple! We are wisely wary of the power of social media apps, and most of us have heard about affairs that started online as people reconnected with old flames, but David and Terri warn couples that actual interaction, *especially at the gym*, can be even more dangerous. If you can't go to the gym *together* as a couple, at least maintain firm boundaries with the people you work out with.

If your marriage is already in a depleted state, with little to no connection, it's foolish to hang around someone of the opposite sex at a time when your brain is vulnerable to a more intense connection. Working out to the point of emotional vulnerability, having someone touch you (just to fix your posture, of course) and encourage you ("Keep going! You got this!"), sets you up to go where you'd never imagine going. Be *honest* about your vulnerability. If you're feeling sexually deprived or emotionally abandoned and putting yourself in harm's way at just the point when you need to keep your defenses keenly on alert, you're ripping down the walls of your fortress and all but inviting an attack.

Next, find refuge in the truth. Reject all secrets. David counsels, "There should be no secret texting, no hesitancy to share passwords to email or social media accounts or cell phones." If you are emotionally hungry, feeling sexually deprived, and secretly communicating with someone who is not your spouse, *you're already having an affair*; it just hasn't become sexual yet.

You don't have to be naked to betray your spouse.

An important caveat about sharing passwords. This teaching doesn't apply to marriages in which abuse is present. There's a difference between hiding from your spouse to cheat on your vows and protecting yourself from being abused or controlled in a threatening or domineering way. A licensed counselor can help you determine whether this piece of advice is wise for your own marriage.

Another "ball" you need to protect your spouse from may be a family member or friend. Terri knows of one woman who earnestly wanted to rebuild her marriage while her husband was ignoring her, but her mother was the primary temptation, constantly telling her, "Why stick with him? You can do so much better. Just leave him already."

"Girlfriends are probably predisposed to take your side a little too quickly," Terri says. "You need to find some mature friends who don't believe a marriage needs to end just because you're in an unhappy place."

Make your marriage a fortress by fortifying your defenses with wise counsel. David points to two people who most inspired him to rebuild his marriage. "My mom shocked me when she said, 'David, if I could go back to when your father cheated on me, I would have hung in there. Terri's affair doesn't have to bring your marriage to an end. It's okay to stay married after an affair. So many people act like staying after an affair is excusing it, but it's not.'" Believing that an affair doesn't have to be fatal can lead you to repair the damage instead of abandoning the ship. Not every heart attack is fatal; sometimes it leads to surgery, which allows the patient to live for many more years. Marriage can be like that.

Remember how Terri's father helped David connect with God by giving him a Bible? He later shocked David when he told him of an early emotional affair in his own marriage. He and Terri's mother had such a deep and mature love that David could hardly believe it was built in the aftermath of betrayal. At first he wanted to ask, "Is there any couple who *hasn't* had an affair of some type?" but eventually even this knowledge brought a fresh infusion of hope. If Terri's parents, the very model of an intimate, devoted, supportive, and happy marriage, could have survived such a serious breach of trust, perhaps he and Terri could as well. "When I saw the current state of their marriage, I knew couples could still thrive after an affair."

TODAY

Terri almost sounds like a schoolgirl with a crush when she tells me, "This past year has been the best year of our thirty-year marriage by far!" For the record, she was referring to 2020, perhaps one of the most infamous years since the Second World War.

"When travel was shut down, it helped us be even more intentional about our relationship, including the importance of dating again."

This is such a crucial point that I want to pause to emphasize it. Recovering from an affair or broken trust isn't a onetime decision; it's a continual process of choosing to grow your marriage. When I ran marathons to qualify for Boston and had to be hyperfocused on my splits, there were six or seven points in every race when I had to decide, once again, *Do I still want to do this?* It's one thing to have intention and resolve at the starting line, or even when you hit the halfway mark. If you want to qualify for Boston, you have to keep deciding to push yourself all the way to the finish line.

In the same way, you don't make one decision to recover from betrayal. You have to keep deciding. Your decision to forgive will be tested. Your decision to go back to what was once a lonely marriage may be terrifying. Your decision to trust again may feel foolish. Your commitment to emotional availability may seem scary. Your ongoing choice to respond sensitively may seem unfair. You will notice some of the same old patterns settling in, and you'll have to decide yet again to act with courage and resolve: "Yes, we're going to keep doing this. We're not just going to survive; we're going to thrive."

Even given all that Terri and David had learned about each other and marriage, it took a worldwide quarantine to remind them that they needed to keep being intentional about their relationship. Having been healed once doesn't mean your marriage can't get sick again.

Working on the "active dating" concept briefly discussed above, David and Terri purposefully do activities on their dates that will keep their heart rates up. The same neurobiological phenomenon that makes working out with your CrossFit trainer dangerous is what can make working out with your spouse a brain hack for better connectivity.

Their strategy for active dating can be as simple as a brisk walk, as exacting as rafting, or as creative as buying tickets to baseball games on the third or first base lines so they have to watch out for foul balls. Excitement and elevated heart rates can do wonders for intimacy enhancement. Maybe it's no accident when high school dates fall in love on roller coasters and carnival rides.

An understanding of this phenomenon has led Terri and David to found Marriage Life Ministries. David explains:

> After a morning of teaching about healthy conflict resolution, we stimulate conflict in the afternoon by strapping couples to a harness system, put them on a tightrope fifty feet in the air, and ask them to navigate an obstacle course together, high up in the canopy of the trees. Just being up high means their heart rates will get above ninety-five beats a minute, which will put them in the fight/flight/freeze mode, and they'll have to employ what we just taught them: deep breaths, looking into each other's eyes, comforting each other, and using God's Word to encourage each other. Couples who go through an adventure-based marital program are 84 percent more likely to sustain the incremental improvements to their marriage.

When it comes to making your marriage a fortress, another benefit of active dating is that it creates positive shared memories that can overcome the hurts of the past. When painful memories arise, a couple can shift to the time when, high up in the air, the husband was there for his wife and the wife was there for her husband. She may have cheated on him years ago, but she held his hand when he started to slip on that retreat. He may have made a large purchase he shouldn't have, but he helped to guide them through those river rapids with a steady hand.

Terri explains, "You have to keep moving forward to get beyond the past. As long as you live in bitterness and unforgiveness, you remain a captive and you lose all hope."

Replacing past pain with present memories has been crucial for David as he continues to offer forgiveness to his wife. "Philippians 4:8 remains a key verse for me: 'Finally, brothers and sisters, whatever is true, whatever is noble, whatever is right, whatever is pure, whatever is lovely, whatever is admirable—if anything is excellent or praiseworthy—think about such things.'"

In his study of neuropsychology, David came across research, based on MRI scans, suggesting that men hold on to anger and resentment for up to six times longer than women, which is why it might be more difficult for men to get over their wives' affairs than it typically is for women to get over their husbands'.

The researchers found that when the aggrieved men looked into an LCD monitor and saw pictures of puppy dogs, deer drinking by a stream, or mountain vistas, their brains would come back to a state of equilibrium.

"I was thinking to myself, *Where have I heard this before?* and I realized it's Philippians 4:8! Think about what is lovely and pure and admirable and noble."

Early on, after Terri confessed to her affair and David was fighting depression, one of the things he did to help him dwell on the positive was to create a playlist of 1970s love songs. He played them every morning as he got ready for work. "As I listened to each of these love songs, I imagined me singing these songs to Terri. Amazingly, with God's help, this technique helped me see my wife differently instead of through my filter of bitterness, resentment, and unforgiveness." It proved so helpful that David continues this practice today. "As a result, I've learned to cherish my wife and intentionally refuse to dwell on the times when she has fallen short of my expectations."[24]

In addition to music, fortify yourself with your favorite photo of your spouse. Put it in a place where you see it every day. It might be sexy; it might be joyful; they might be laughing or look pensive—whatever makes you fall in love with them again. And then remind yourself of their favorite traits.

On top of that, get your heart rate up and build positive memories, adding to the list every week. Make sex sensuous again, build all five levels of intimacy, and your marriage can once again become an impregnable fortress against any kind of marital affair or betrayal.

Remember the three elements that can especially lead to reattachment: *emotional availability*, *sensitive responsiveness*, and *trust*. Make yourself available to your spouse by being sensitive to what they are saying and feeling. A consistent pattern of being available, sensitive, and responsive leads to greater trust. Greater trust leads to feelings of safety, which lead to feelings of emotional attachment.

> Turn your ear to me,
>   come quickly to my rescue;
> be my rock of refuge,
>   a strong fortress to save me. (Psalm 31:2)

Building Your Fortress Takeaways

1. Emotional connection or attachment keeps marriages strong through trials. No matter what is trying to tear you apart, focus on keeping attached and connected emotionally.

2. The building blocks of emotional attachment are emotional availability, sensitive responsiveness, and trust.

3. Betrayal is to a marriage what dynamite is to a door. It threatens to blow apart everything the two of you have worked to build.

4. God, the author and finisher of our faith, is working to bring us back together, even as our own actions threaten to tear us apart.

5. A couple can all but hate each other one year and then, through growth, change, and faith, learn to cherish and delight in each other.

6. Affairs are frequently gradual, entered into through many little steps. In time, little steps can carry us a long way, which is why we want to be careful about taking the first step in the wrong direction.

7. Spiritual rehabilitation doesn't make marital rehabilitation automatic. You still have to rebuild emotional availability, sensitive responsiveness, and trust.

8. In the midst of David's pain over what his wife had done, he found healing by being sensitive to God's voice reminding him what *he* had done and what *he*

needed to change. Your spouse's sin doesn't excuse your own.

9. Unaddressed childhood wounds, unrealistic expectations, and failure to prioritize marriage can make you especially susceptible to an affair.

10. Emotional disconnection doesn't require marital earthquakes. It can result from slow, steady, and relatively small acts of apathy and disconnection that eventually combine to create a huge divide.

11. According to David and Terri, the five layers of intimacy are spiritual, sexual, sensual, emotional, and intellectual.

12. Just because a couple is still having sex doesn't necessarily mean everything is okay. Pay attention to the *kind* of sex you're having. Is it about connecting, giving to each other, and enjoying each other, or is it about using each other to meet your physical needs? Sexuality divorced from sensuality is a serious red flag.

13. It's possible to experience a deeper level of intimacy and satisfaction after an affair or betrayal than what you had before the affair.

14. Transparency on all levels is essential for continued emotional attachment as long as it's safe for each spouse.

15. Elevated heart rates put our brains in a heightened state of emotion, which can lead to increased marital intimacy or make us more vulnerable to an affair.

16. When you seek counsel about your marriage, talk to people with biblical values who trust in the Lord's power and grace.

17. The choice to recover from betrayal isn't a onetime decision or a decision one person can make alone. Recovery from betrayal is a continual process of two people choosing to grow their marriage.

18. Having been healed once doesn't mean your marriage can't get sick again. We have to keep growing our marriage even after renewal so we can combat any drift toward emotional detachment.

19. Active dating helps you replace thoughts of past betrayal with new memories of shared trust.

CHAPTER 5
· · · · · · · · · · · · · · · ·

TOO BUSY TO CONNECT
AND CARE

Becoming a Relationally
Industrious Couple

T he reason a sucker punch succeeds isn't always related to its
force; more often than not, it is about surprise. The person
doesn't see it coming. The victim isn't prepared. The punch is
totally unexpected and undefended. That's what allows it to do
maximum damage. Take away the surprise, and a sucker punch,
by definition, is no longer a sucker punch; it's just a problem you
can prepare for.

Busyness may be the biggest sucker punch marriages face
today. Couples know to look out for an affair. They have been
warned that when they lose a child to death or give birth to a
child with disabilities, their marriage becomes newly vulnerable.
They've heard the statistics about what these challenges can do

to their marriage, and they want to guard against adding to those numbers.

Busyness that lulls us to sleep before it punches us can be every bit as deadly as any other major assault. It doesn't even sound like an assault. Saying busyness is a threat is a bit like saying driving is dangerous. We know it, but we assume it's dangerous for others, not for us. In any given year, more than two million drivers in the United States alone will be injured in an automobile accident. More than thirty thousand will die of their injuries. But nobody expects it will happen to them on any particular trip.

Until it does.

At first, overly busy people simply lose their edge, their ability to cherish the other person. Overly busy people have a difficult time appreciating each other and cherishing each other because they're so tired and so distracted by everything they're scrambling to get done. Then they start to feel irritated with each other and taken for granted. Then they start to feel lonely—*Why won't my spouse help me and make my life better?* Then they start to feel angry because they hate the situation they're in. Hating the situation you're in with your spouse is but one small step from hating your spouse.

And that's when the sucker punch lands.

Will it be a knockout?

Randy is a senior pastor in Vernon, British Columbia, and Hannah is a music teacher. They've been married for twenty-five years and have two teens and a preteen. Anyone who has experienced that season of child-rearing knows you can spell those years as the b-u-s-y years. Yet they've found a way to fight back by becoming what I call a "relationally industrious" couple—two people who intentionally apply and refine relationship skills to keep growing their marriage through the various seasons of life.

Surely you've heard about the second law of thermodynamics. A very amateur definition inexpertly applied to relationships is that if you don't have positive movement in a forward direction, deterioration and retreat are certain. Left on their own, things naturally fall apart. This means that even to keep our marriage at the same level of intimacy requires intentional forward progress. If we don't *grow* in our relationship skills, we'll *retreat* in our marital satisfaction. Much of our thinking these days is based on asking the question, "Are we a good match?" But the better question after we get married (since the match is already made) is, "Are we a *skilled* couple?" With the exception of death or divorce, you can't change who you're married to, but you can change your marital skills, which will give you a new marriage on many levels. I've seen it happen many times.

Drs. Les and Leslie Parrott talk about this in *I Love You More*: "Experts have found that the majority of couples could significantly improve their marriage by simply learning one new skill for better handling their major deficiency. Research backs it up and practice bears it out: We all need new skills to make marriage work well."[25]

If we would adopt the intention and take the time to grow one new relational skill each year (listening, empathy, humility, emotional attachment, conflict resolution, sexual intimacy, and so forth), our marriage would become stronger. You may already be highly skilled relationally, but consider this—even professional athletes, the best competitors in the world, keep practicing so they can improve their skills and even add new skills so their opponents don't surpass them. If you want a better marriage, become more skilled at marriage! As the Parrots write, "You may be thinking that you don't have any deficiencies. If so, that's probably your biggest deficiency! . . . *Every* marriage has a deficiency. It may be different for every couple, but be assured that every couple has one."[26]

How is this connected to busyness? Marriage just doesn't seem as urgent as a job crisis or the kids' schedule. Your boss may fire you if you don't reach your sales quota, but will your spouse divorce you if you don't become a slightly better listener? Probably not. So we gravitate toward the urgent until we reach the point where we forget to work on our relational skills.

And that's when the sucker punch lands.

Some important relational skills we need to keep on refining are listening to the voice and counsel of God, growing in empathy, practicing conflict resolution, working on our communication, exploring our love languages, cherishing each other, listening to each other, doing regular relationship check-ins, having fun together, and pursuing enhanced sexual intimacy. Seek to grow in these skills whenever you see any of them beginning to wane. If you're too busy to seek growth in these areas, you're too busy! Satan is most likely to attack your marriage exactly where you are most negligent. Ignoring relational skills or letting them become rusty is like building a ten-foot-tall metal door at the front of your castle while neglecting a large, gaping hole in the side wall. We don't get to choose where our enemy decides to attack.

SPIRITUAL DISCERNMENT AND EMPATHY

Like so many couples I've talked to, Hannah and Randy were doing fine until they weren't. A new and unexpected situation—worldwide shutdowns due to COVID-19—launched unanticipated challenges. Hannah explains, "When Randy gets busy, he fixes his mind on what's happening in his vocational life—what to do about it and how to fix it. That happened in 2020 when our church initiated online services after COVID-19 hit. And I could tell just by looking at him that there was no mind space left over for me. Unlike so many husbands, Randy spent *more* hours away from home during the pandemic, and even when he was home, he was just paying me lip service."

Randy became fixated on making Sunday online services better. He sensed the services weren't what they needed to be, and when he realized that COVID-19 was unleashing a much longer shutdown than people had originally thought, he wasn't content with just getting by.

Hannah felt angry because "the services were already really good, but Randy constantly wanted to take more time to make them even better. I wanted him to put some of his energy toward connection with me and our family."

They decided to go paddleboarding. While they were on the lake, an older couple they knew and respected pulled up in a ski boat. The wife said, "It's such a romantic, lovely date night!"

Hannah responded, "Actually, we're not even speaking right now, so not so romantic."

The couple invited them to come to their house, and they had some good honest conversation about the connection and time management issues Randy and Hannah were struggling with. Hannah admits that many emotions were shared that weren't so helpful, but after a night's rest, the Holy Spirit boiled down the conversation, and Hannah was able to see that Randy was carrying a huge load on his shoulders. The extra work was only for a season, and he hadn't neglected Hannah or their family on purpose. Randy was able to hear and understand Hannah's perspective and agreed to be more aware of his time and mind space.

WHO NEEDS TO HEAR WHAT?

I want to pause here to address other couples who face this challenge of being too busy to connect, especially when it's a little more one-sided. When you are very frustrated with your spouse, you naturally want to talk to them. You want to be heard. You want your spouse to understand what's bugging you. That desire is legitimate, but just as much as your spouse needs to hear from you, *you need to hear from the Holy Spirit*. You may not welcome the thoughts that float into your mind or the advice of trusted friends, but if you live by the motto "I need to hear from the Holy Spirit more than my spouse needs to hear from me," you're on the path to relational and spiritual health.

I believe Christianity is a supernatural faith. One of the most important relational skills to cultivate is the ability to become more and more open to and familiar with the leading, presence, and counsel of a supernatural God. Go through a Bible concordance and notice how many times God tells his people to "listen." It's a pattern in Jesus' teaching.

"Listen and understand" (Matthew 15:10).

"Jesus called the crowd to him and said, 'Listen to me, everyone, and understand this'" (Mark 7:14).

Jesus said spiritual understanding is dependent on this one skill: "Therefore consider carefully how you listen" (Luke 8:18).

When God let Peter, James, and John see Jesus transfigured before them, what's the one thing God told this blessed trio? "This is my Son, whom I love; with him I am well pleased. *Listen* to him!" (Matthew 17:5, emphasis added).

After Jesus' death and resurrection, God gave us his Holy Spirit as our comforter and advocate (John 14:26). He leads us into all truth (John 14:17; 16:13). Let's not assume we see ourselves and our spouse as we and they truly are. James 1:5 specifically tells us that if we lack wisdom, we need to ask God for it, and it will be given to us. The Holy Spirit may then tell us to keep pressing the issue with our spouse—who knows? But let's listen *first*.[27]

When you're hurting, it's good to have someone hear you out. You want your spouse to hear your frustrations. You want your friends to understand your pain. You want your counselor to perceive your challenges. But more than all of this, you need to hear from God.

Jesus warned that our natural response is to look at the speck of sawdust in our neighbor's eye while we have a log in our own.[28] His point likely elicited chuckles from the crowd. When we silently protest, "But my spouse really *does* have a speck in their eye," just know *you're exactly the person Jesus is challenging.* You have adopted the mindset that Jesus says to reject.

Marital reconciliation begins when we admit, "I need to hear from the Holy Spirit more than my spouse needs to hear from me."

Fortunately, Hannah adopted that attitude, and though she wasn't convinced by the advice she had been given the night before, "the next morning, I realized that all the ways Randy hurt me weren't his fault; he wasn't doing any of it on purpose. And because of that, I didn't want to hold anything against him anymore."

The brilliance of this insight is that Hannah realized the enemy in her marriage wasn't Randy; it was the *situation.* Randy was under a lot of stress, stretched beyond his limits. He wasn't responding as healthily as he could have, but he wasn't in the "space zone" out of spite or apathy or malice. He was simply trying to be a faithful pastor in a critical time.

"I thought he needed to make a big change in our marriage," says Hannah, "but I also realized that his heart is good and well intentioned toward me. Out of that admission, I was able to release him from judgment."

The relational skill she put into play here is empathy.[29] If you're experiencing emotional disconnection from your spouse, before you evaluate your spouse, *evaluate the situation they are facing.* Is it really the case that your spouse doesn't care? Or is it possible that your spouse is facing a situation they just can't handle or don't know how to handle? Ask yourself, *In my frustration over how my spouse is treating me, how can I have empathy for the way life is treating my spouse?* (Of course, this is *not* meant to excuse abuse.)[30]

According to Dr. Les Parrott, "Research has shown that 90 percent of our struggles in marriage would be resolved if we did nothing more than see that problem from our partner's perspective."[31]

Empathy won't solve your and your spouse's problems, but it will help keep you emotionally connected. And being emotionally connected as you face your problems together is, in the end, more important than having your problems solved. Isn't marriage about living life together even more than it's about having a perfect life alone?

SIGNS OF TROUBLE

What are the symptoms of "overbusyness" as a couple? The reason it's especially important to become aware of these symptoms is that some couples notice emotional estrangement and blame it on their *pairing* rather than on the *situation*. Two well-matched people can become estranged, but by improving their skills and empathy, they can come back together stronger and be more intimate than ever. Romanticism tempts us to think that if we don't feel close, we must no longer be a fit. Emotional satisfaction in marriage isn't about the fit; it's about the connection.

In this chapter, I'm addressing the *situation* so that it doesn't annihilate the *relationship*. Stop evaluating your fit. You've already made your choice! Focus all your energy on re-establishing your connection.

Hannah and Randy know that they are too busy, Hannah says, "when we can't make eye contact and understand each other. He doesn't know what's going on with me and I don't know what's going on with him."

I like this model of defining " too busy" by relational awareness. It's not really about their schedules or even about the amount of time they are spending together; it's about whether or not they're *connected*. Would you be able to tell me your spouse's current greatest temptation, frustration, and fear? Could you tell me what they long for in the next week, the next month, the next year? Without asking and listening, we gradually become strangers to our spouse's struggles, hurts, disappointments, and fears—and that makes them feel alone and abandoned.

"It's important to me," says Hannah, "that when he looks at me, he has a clue about what's going on with me and vice versa—that I know what's going on with him."

Of course, it's not just Randy who occasionally gets into the "space zone." Hannah has her moments as well. Randy explains, "Contrary to the male stereotype, I'm less of a linear thinker and will want to talk things out. That means I can ramble sometimes, and Hannah may respond with, 'What are you getting at? We don't have time for this. Just make your point.' It's not easy for me to bring something up in the moment. I have to process it. That's why Tuesday nights are so important for us; it gives me time, which gives me perspective."

They don't just wait for Tuesday evenings, however. "We need to have time every morning and evening to make that connection," Randy explains. "I'll bring Hannah her coffee in the morning when she first gets up, but I've learned that she doesn't want me to sit by her right away. She needs some time alone. I'll come in later with the second cup of coffee and ask what's going on with her day, and that's when we'll connect. It takes just five or ten minutes, but without that small investment, we feel disconnected."

Hannah seems to be more sensitive to relational disconnect than Randy, so he's learned to let her be the relational thermometer. She says, "Randy is more of a physical connector, but when there isn't a relational and emotional connection, I'm not offering much of a physical connection."

This is exactly the point that divides so many couples. The husband wants more physical intimacy; the wife wants more emotional connection (though the reverse can be true as well). And what happens is that because the wife feels cheated emotionally (you've heard this a million times), she pulls back from the husband physically. And because the husband feels cheated physically, he pulls back emotionally—and the problem keeps getting worse.

Here's why the opposite happens for Randy and Hannah, and why this dynamic makes their marriage a fortress instead of reducing it to ruins. *They both value connection.* They have different barometers of connection, but instead of resenting how disconnection feels to them, it wakes them up to the fact that they need to reconnect. If married couples would learn to let these differences draw them together instead of pulling them apart, they would have much happier relationships.

It begins, though, when both partners value being connected. A husband who just wants to have sex or a wife who just wants to talk without caring whether the other feels connected doesn't want relational health; they just want their own needs met. You can see how, in a healthy marriage, two different barometers (physical intimacy and emotional intimacy) can serve as two different warning lights rather than being seen as two different arguments. It's almost like a fail-safe system.

Randy and Hannah's push for connection is in keeping with science. Dr. Archibald Hart and Dr. Sharon May write, "The number one predictor for divorce is *emotional disconnection*, not fighting."[32] Which means if you avoid fights (we're not speaking about physical fights, of course) because you're afraid they might crater your marriage, you may be doing more harm to your marriage. Conflict avoidance often leads to emotional disconnection.

Hannah explains, "We always teach couples three things: date night, consistent time devoted to talking about their marriage, and a regular business meeting where they discuss finances and their schedules."

For Randy and Hannah, the "business meetings" usually take place in the morning. Tuesday nights are for reconnecting. And yes, there's some pushback. Hannah says, "Sometimes our kids get mad. 'Are you going out *again*?' I just say, 'Yes! We need to go learn to love each other better. Don't you want us to stay married after you leave?'"

Date nights sometimes include discussion, and sometimes they don't. "We have to be careful," Randy warns, "because if conflict comes up, the date night can be shot."

He remembers "the most beautiful sunset I've ever seen in Vancouver"—an evening made for romance—"and we wrecked it with an awful disagreement. That's why you need relational time separate from date nights. If you always wait until date nights to reconnect, you can ruin those special nights. We try to keep date nights all about nurturing our relationship and friendship."

A person training for a marathon typically does some easy recovery runs, some speedwork, and some endurance runs. The best training schedule seeks to incorporate all three, but *not on the same day*. Marital fitness requires the same broad view. Sometimes we have to take care of business. Sometimes we have to just sit and talk. Sometimes sexual intimacy can serve the relationship. Trying to do all three on the same night is like trying to balance ten spinning plates at one time.

NO FAKING ALLOWED

Randy knows there's a problem with their connection if he moves in for a hug and Hannah instinctively pulls away.

"If I'm feeling emotionally disconnected, I can't fake it," Hannah explains. "If Randy protests, 'Come on, I'm just trying to give you a hug,' it doesn't matter. When we are running at a breakneck pace and haven't been connecting, I can't get physical."

Randy doesn't take this personally. Instead, he asks himself, *Did we miss our last date night? Are we scrimping on our heart-to-hearts in the morning?* Rather than lash out at the symptoms of emotional disconnection, he seeks to find the cause. He actually likes the fact that Hannah isn't good at faking.

Hannah explains, "I *can't* act all lovey-dovey and touchy if we're not connecting relationally."

Randy chimes in, "I hear marriage speakers say to women, 'You've got to do your duty for your man regardless,' but I'm glad Hannah isn't that way."

Hannah explains why: "At least he knows when I'm physical with him, it's authentic and real, which makes it more meaningful for both of us. We read this book about what a man needs and what a woman needs, and that if the man will do some things, the woman will respond sexually—" and then she pauses. "Wait, you didn't write that book, did you?"

"No."

"Okay, good. Because it doesn't work that way for us. I'm not good at faking it, and Randy doesn't want me to fake it. The notion that a wife just has to meet her husband's sexual needs so that he starts meeting her emotional needs doesn't work for us. We're striving for *real* intimacy in our marriage. I don't want *pretend* intimacy."

Randy offers an important caveat: "Everything doesn't have to be perfect in our relationship for Hannah to want to be physical. She's not looking for an excuse to avoid me in the bedroom. She just doesn't want to pretend we're connected when we're not, and I respect that."

Randy adds that when a couple stops being physically intimate and a lack of emotional connection follows, the couple may start fighting about the wrong things—namely, sex and communication. But it's not about that. It's really about respect and connection. "The guy says, 'I'm not feeling respected. I'm doing all this work but she wants more; what more can I give her? I don't have time to do whatever more she needs. I can't do more work around the house.' But that may not be what she needs; she just wants to bond. What you do around the house and what she does in the bedroom are often signs of something deeper."

Let me pause here, because this is a key point: *make sure you know what you're really fighting about.* A fight about who does most of the chores can really be about whether the wife feels estranged from the husband and the husband feels frustrated because there's so little sex. Chores and sex become the focal point, but they're the symptoms, not what really bothers each partner. More than she wants the counters cleaned, the wife may want to know the husband sees her, cares about her, has empathy for her, and doesn't take her for granted. More than the husband cares about being confronted, he wants to know she sees his hard work, appreciates his commitment, and doesn't see him as some sort of utilitarian, take-care-of-me robot.

When there's emotional connection, the husband doesn't want to frustrate his wife and the wife doesn't want to harp at her husband. Go deeper in your discussion. Is this really about a toilet seat, or is it mostly about a relational breakdown? Unleash the relational skills of communication and listening.

BY DEGREES

To make your marriage a fortress against this common challenge of busyness, it's crucial to remember that relational estrangement happens slowly, by degrees. Shortly before I turned fifty, I moved to a new state (Texas) and essentially started working two jobs. Since I was a recent empty nester, I had the ability to let my work hours go way up, and they did. The Texas climate wasn't conducive to running off my sweet-tooth indulgences. To no one's surprise, I started to gain some weight.

Just a little. Maybe a quarter pound a week.

But a quarter pound a week becomes a pound a month. A pound a month becomes twelve pounds a year. Twelve pounds in a year becomes twenty-five pounds in two years.

I woke up one January 1, stepped on the scale, and saw a number I'd never seen before. *What just happened?* I asked.

Nothing *just* happened. Something *did* happen slowly and steadily.

Relationally, estrangement is just like that. You're a "little" too busy. You start watching a "little" more television. You spend a "little" more time apart. You spend a "little" less time having sex. You spend a "little" more time with the kids or at your job than you do with each other. You slowly, with glacier-like steadiness, grow a "little" more apart.

After a period of time, those "littles" become a big sum—to the point where you may not even like each other very much.

It's important to remember that you can address the situation without torpedoing the relationship. When our heavy bathroom door starts squeaking, I don't tear the door off and buy a new one. I spray a little WD-40 on the hinges, and it's good for another six months. We need the same attitude in our marriage. We can fix those squeaks and irritants without scrapping the entire marriage.

Randy and Hannah make their marriage a fortress by asking the right questions that enable them to go deeper. Randy asks himself, *Why am I annoyed with Hannah? Why is she annoyed with me?* They work hard to make sure *annoyance* doesn't lead to *contempt*.

Hannah explains, "Being able to carve out time to be alone is the only cure to being unable to connect. If you're not connecting, of course you're not going to feel in love anymore." Randy adds, "I don't like the phrase 'too busy to bond.' We're not too busy. There's enough time. If you're feeling emotionally taxed or tired and exhausted, it's because you're putting something above your marriage. Let's be honest, when I start carrying too much stuff at work, I'm taking it out of my marriage."

Let me repeat this phrase, as it highlights the "sucker punch" that takes so many marriages by surprise: *When I start carrying too much stuff at work, I'm taking it out of my marriage.* For "work" you could substitute "parenting," "extended family," "hobby," or something else. Time and energy are finite. Something has to give.

When Randy's church services went online, he and his staff had to reinvent Sunday morning in a way that would keep church members engaged. No seminary course covered this topic, but the suddenness with which in-person church services came to an end meant he had no time to learn. He was online just days after finding out the building would be empty on Sundays going forward.

Naturally, going online would take focus, energy, and passion. Nobody has unlimited focus, energy, and passion, which meant that Hannah got less of each. And that new expenditure of focus, energy, and passion made Randy tired in a way he had never been tired before.

"But I can't say there wasn't time," Randy admits. "There *was* time. I no longer had a commute. But I was also mentally tired in a new way, and when you're mentally tired, it's easier to turn on Netflix than to have a deep conversation."

Hannah adds, "It's a huge red flag if you'd rather scroll through social media than have a conversation with your spouse."

A PATTERN OF TRIAL AND SUCCESS

How often do Randy and Hannah find themselves going through cycles of busyness? "It depends on the season," Hannah explains. "As a teacher, I don't work in the summer, so there's much less strain on our marriage then, and we seem to have a better connection in the summer. When we're both working, we need to autocorrect every six to eight weeks."

Autocorrecting is a lot of work. People see the results but not the process, and they sometimes assume the good results are because Randy and Hannah are a good match rather than acknowledging the hard work they put into their relationship. "Our friends get upset with us because, well, we do marriage seminars. Based on the way we present ourselves in ministry, they think we have a great marriage that's just been given to us—the best they've ever seen—but they don't realize how hard we have to work at it. They don't believe it when we say we need to come back together to focus and intentionally reconnect regularly."

I want to underscore this. Randy and Hannah have a deep connection, not because they are a naturally good match, but because they are relationally industrious. They are intentional. They search their own hearts. They strive to reconnect. They care about making sure each of them feels connected. They spend time together, which means that they'll sometimes have to say no to other things, including their children and their vocations.

Why put in the work to keep doing seeking reconnection? Is it really worth it?

Hannah laughs. "We're in it for the long haul. Who wants to be miserable for the long haul?"

MAKING **YOUR MARRIAGE** A FORTRESS

They know they're going to be married for a long time. So they asked themselves, *Would we rather be happily married or frustrated in our marriage? Why not put in a bit more work to stay closer to the happy side?*

Randy adds, "We're simply not content to live in a disconnected way. And now, with more experience, we can see disconnection coming in certain seasons. As we talk over our schedules or new commitments, we'll say something like, 'If you take on this and I take on that, well, we know where that's going to lead. Are we taking on too much?'"

It's not just subjective though. In addition to Tuesday nights and morning and evening connections, they set regular goals. Hannah explains, "We try to get away from the kids two or three nights twice a year. Doing so hits the reset button. We've been fortunate in that my parents are willing to be with the kids. The reason it needs to be two or three nights is that sometimes it takes twenty-four hours away before we've gotten to know each other again and remember why we love each other."

THE RELATIONAL SOLUTION

A valuable exercise that helps Randy and Hannah stay connected is their "Tuesday in-house date night." They take turns planning them. One night, Hannah set up a tent with sheets for the roof. Another night, Randy set up tarps in their garage and put up a large painting canvas, and they created a splatter paint studio.

The struggle to make these nights happen creates cherished memories. Hannah is particularly fond of the splatter paint night. "That was the best. It was really great because we were waiting *forever* to get the kids in bed. Randy kept looking outside, and it frustrated me because I wanted him to help, not be distracted. I didn't know why he was so focused on the garage, only to find out he had lit a bunch of candles and was worried the garage was going to burn down! I think it was nine or nine thirty before we got out there."

When their kids didn't go to sleep right away on those in-house date nights, it would have been so easy just to say, "Maybe another night," and go to bed. But that wasn't what Randy and Hannah did. Hannah says, "We're intentional about something that gets us in each other's mind space and builds joy. We handle responsibility so differently that marriage becomes joyless if we only focus on the responsibilities. We need to step away from our responsibilities, recognize our relationship, and enjoy it."

Oh, and yes, they still have their completed splatter paint canvas.

THE SPIRITUAL SOLUTION

Often marital relational disconnection has its spiritual roots in our relationship with God. Randy explains, "A big part of this isn't just between the two of you. It's about you before God. Are you feeling like a whole person? If not, you're just grabbing from your partner. If you're desperate for what your partner can give you, are you too busy to bond with God first?"

Connection with God in marriage has been the main focus of my writing and teaching, beginning with *Sacred Marriage*. Some people feel disconnected from God and blame the ensuing listlessness on their spouse. They start asking too much of their spouse. It's possible to fall off on either end—ignoring each other and becoming disconnected or depending too much on each other and becoming disappointed.

To keep the spiritual temperature rising in their marriage, Randy and Hannah are fans of putting Bible verses on their bathroom mirror. One of Randy's favorites is Nehemiah 8:10: "The joy of the LORD is my strength." He explains, "The Lord's joy is a gift offered to me. I don't have to require that from Hannah; it's *God's* joy that is my strength."

Hannah revels in Lamentations 3:22–23 (ESV): "'The steadfast love of the LORD never ceases; his mercies never come to an end; they are new every morning; great is your faithfulness.' That verse is big for me because I want to start with new grace for Randy every morning."

Their life verse is Ephesians 5:21: "Submit to one another out of reverence for Christ." The reason this is such a stellar marital life verse is that it calls both husband and wife to submit to each other's need to connect.

"To submit, you must commit," Randy explains. "It goes both ways. When a husband asks, 'Why are you harping on me when I'm already working so hard?' he's not submitting to his wife's desire to connect; he's resenting her desire to connect. Maybe she'd rather he work a little less hard at his job and a little harder at their relationship."

This idea of needing to "submit to commit" goes far beyond schedules. When I work with younger couples and hear from a wife who is anxious about her husband staying connected to a former girlfriend on Facebook, my first question to the husband is, "Why would you keep doing something you know bugs your wife? How will doing that make her feel connected to you?" Some wives don't care about these things, but if your wife does care, it doesn't help when you survey your small group to gain ammunition to contend that your wife is being too sensitive. The truth is, if you want to feel connected with your wife, *her opinion is the only one that matters.* That mindset—submitting to each other out of reverence for Christ—is a great way to keep your marriage on track.[33]

THREE FLIPS A DAY

I have an hourglass that helps me focus my most intense creative work. To make sure I'm prioritizing the best things over the good things, I'm committed to engaging in intense creative work for at least three flips a day.

When I used this as a sermon illustration once, I was surprised by how many people asked where they could get an hourglass like mine.

Apparently, I'm not the only one who needs help focusing on what's most important.

If you want to make your marriage a fortress, *you must build time for each other.* You'll never discover time. It will rarely fall into your lap—voila, you've been given three unexpected hours to work on your marriage. You must prioritize it and make it happen.

Marriage is like so many other things. For example, you don't just wake up one day in good enough shape to climb a mountain; you train three or four days a week for a few months to get there. The same is true for marital fitness. It has to become a priority.

Justin noticed this with Lauren. In the midst of an ongoing issue with one of their children, they just weren't connecting. Justin found himself plagued with fantasies, sometimes sexual, sometimes even emotional. When it came down to it, he just wanted a more pleasant marriage and wondered what it might be like if he was married to a woman who was a little more laid-back than his take-charge, firstborn, sometimes emotionally distant wife.

Justin told me:

> God doesn't usually speak directly enough to me that I know it's him talking, but this time, while I was praying, I felt a warning and very specific directives, more clearly than perhaps I've ever heard before. The fantasies were taking me down a dangerous road—not just a dead-end road but a dangerous road. Instead of engaging in fantasies, I needed to do three things: pray with my wife every day, take her on a date night once a week, and make a bigger effort in the bedroom. We had fallen into routine in all three of those areas, and God made it clear to me that I needed to step up the emotional, spiritual, and sexual components of our marriage.

God was calling Justin to be more relationally industrious. Having three things to focus on worked well for Justin:

> Prayer was pretty easy. Before we went to sleep, I asked Lauren how I could pray for her. Earlier in the day when something came up, I just said, "Let's pray about that."
>
> The date night thing surprised her. She pushed back a little bit at first, but after a few weeks, it became our new routine. One week, we had a child emergency and had to cancel our plans, and Lauren looked at me and said, "I'm really disappointed. I'm going to miss our night tonight."

For the sexual component, I actually used one of your blog posts. "What do you think about this post?" I asked, and I invited her to read it. Just talking about sex heated both of us up. And I think the fact that I was initiating by suggesting something *she* might like made it seem far more "giving" than if I had simply complained about our not having enough sex.

Anyway, the thing I noticed was that focusing on the three things was like unleashing a powerful offense, and the defense took care of itself. The lure of the fantasies was gone. I didn't have enough mental room left over to pursue them *and* pursue my wife, so they just faded away. I'm not a porn guy, but the fantasies still made me feel guilty. Reconnecting with my wife gave me hope.

And one night, I combined all three. We prayed on the way to our date night, which was at a hotel where we had a hot time without any need to be quiet! Looking back, the fantasies were a way I tried to cope with feeling separated from my wife, but they made me feel even *more* separated afterward. It set my marriage on a potential death spiral, and I don't ever want to drift like that again.

Justin ended up taking some of the Bible's best advice without knowing it. Listen to Paul's advice in Ephesians 4:20–24:

That, however, is not the way of life you learned when you heard about Christ and were taught in him in accordance with the truth that is in Jesus. You were taught, with regard to your former way of life, to put off your old self, which is being corrupted by its deceitful desires; to be made new in the attitude of your minds; and to put on the new self, created to be like God in true righteousness and holiness.

I understand that recommending praying together, having a date night, and being more intentional about creativity in the bedroom sounds like the ultimate cliché marriage advice. That's why I almost hesitated to include this real story. But sometimes clichés work. We don't always need magic elixirs or exotic practices. Justin's conclusions made me think of Naaman, the Syrian commander who took offense after he was told by Elisha that his leprosy would be cured if he dipped in the Jordan seven times.[34] Elisha's "cure" seemed too simple. The commander wanted something more complicated, more worthy of his visit.

But we need to remember that God often works through the simple.

If you find yourself in a particularly busy season in which the husband is drifting toward fantasy and the wife is picking up the latest romance novel, why not at least give Justin's "three flips" a try? I don't fault my physician for prescribing a common drug like amoxicillin when I need an antibiotic. I don't say, "Come on, Doc, give me a medicine I've never heard of before to prove to me you know what you're talking about." If amoxicillin works, I would be a fool to ignore it.

In the same way, how are you doing in regard to praying together? Have you stayed consistent with your date nights? Are you applying a little creativity in the bedroom?[35]

There isn't just *one* solution to fight marital drift, but there is a solution for you. Consider which marital skills you lack and become ruthless about pursuing them. Be intentional, thoughtful, and prayerful so your marriage can become a fortress against poor priorities.

> My salvation and my honor depend on God;
> he is my mighty rock, my refuge. (Psalm 62:7)

Building Your Fortress Takeaways

1. Being overly busy is one of the most destructive sucker punches that assaults marriages today. Its danger lies in the fact that we don't always see it as an assault until the damage has been done.

2. So much of today's approach in marriage is based on, "Are we a good match?" But the better question after we are married is, "Are we a *skilled* couple?" Keeping our focus on that question will allow us to grow our relational skills.

3. Some important relational skills are listening to the voice and counsel of God, growing in empathy, practicing conflict resolution, working on our communication, exploring our love languages, cherishing each other, listening to each other, doing regular relationship check-ins, having fun together, and pursuing enhanced sexual intimacy. Seek to grow in these areas on an increasing basis when you see any one of these beginning to wane. If you're too busy to grow these skills, you're too busy!

4. When you're frustrated with your spouse, it's natural to want to be heard and understood. That desire is legitimate, but just as much as your spouse needs to hear from you, you need to hear from the Holy Spirit.

5. When your marriage is under stress due to outside factors and your spouse isn't responding in the best way, try to remember that your spouse isn't the enemy;

the enemy is the *situation* you're trying to combat. Before you evaluate your spouse, evaluate the situation they're in.

6. In your frustration over how your spouse is treating you, how can you have empathy for the way life is treating your spouse? (Note: This does *not* excuse abuse.)

7. Empathy may not solve your and your spouse's problems, but it will help you stay emotionally connected as you face those problems.

8. A relationally industrious couple is an intentional couple who recognizes that new skills must be learned or old skills must be relaunched to face new marital challenges. Instead of passively sitting back, the couple figures out how to draw closer together.

9. Two well-matched people can become estranged, but by improving their skills and empathy, they can come back together stronger and more intimate than ever.

10. Romanticism tempts us to think that if we don't feel close, we must no longer be a fit. Emotional satisfaction in marriage isn't about the fit; it's about the connection.

11. Being too busy is best defined through the lens of relational awareness. Are you aware of what your spouse is feeling and going through?

12. Having different barometers of connection (emotional, physical, or something else) can draw you closer together rather than pull you apart if you pay attention to both of them instead of pitting one against the other.

13. The top predictor for divorce isn't fighting; it's *emotional disconnection*, which means that avoiding arguments because you're afraid they'll crater your marriage may be doing more harm to your marriage. Conflict avoidance can lead to emotional disconnection, which is a greater threat than temporary frustration.

14. To stay connected, Randy and Hannah encourage three kinds of meetings: date night, regular time set aside to talk about your marriage, and a regular business meeting.

15. Rather than lash out at the *symptoms* of emotional disconnection (lack of desire to talk or engage in physical intimacy), seek to find the *cause*.

16. Go deeper in your discussion to determine whether your challenges are really about things like a toilet seat or instead signal a relational breakdown.

17. Relational estrangement happens slowly, by degrees.

18. One of the ways to keep annoyance from slipping into contempt is to ask the "why" questions.

19. Spiritual connection with God—including receiving his love and affirmation every day—helps us stay emotionally connected to our spouse without burying them with our expectations and demands.

20. Submitting to one another out of reverence for Christ is a vital part of staying connected as a couple.

21. Don't be hesitant to try what may seem to be clichéd advice if it works.

CHAPTER 6

WHEN LIBIDOS COLLIDE

Making Sex a Blessing
Instead of a Burden

When sexual intimacy is mutually enjoyable, it becomes part of a marriage's defense against other life assaults; when this intimacy is the main point of contention, it can become a major assault. Good sex can't save a bad marriage, but bad sex can certainly make a marriage vulnerable. Of course, I've seen a number of marriages where sex ceased for health reasons, yet the couples continued to experience close intimacy and passionate attachment. The question often isn't, "How often do you have sex?" but rather, "Why are you or aren't you having sex?" Relationally speaking, the why is often more important than the what.

Since I've already written a book on sexual intimacy in marriage,[36] in this book I want to highlight one of the most common sexual frustrations in marriage—namely, differences in libido. Even if this particular challenge isn't an issue in your marriage, it will serve as a way to address other sexual issues that could pull the two of you apart. I want to make it clear that in this chapter I'm not addressing marriages where abuse or addictions are present. It's not appropriate to address increasing the frequency of sexual intimacy when abuse or betrayal trauma are issues.

EMILY AND FRED

Fred and Emily's first two dates were "pretty much disasters," so Emily suggested for their third date that they go to the airport and "watch airplanes," a euphemism—at least in Emily's mind—for making out in the parking lot next to the runway. As soon as the young couple parked, Emily unbuckled her seatbelt to climb into Fred's lap. He said, "Wait! Hold up! What are you doing?"

Emily was confused. "Um, what are *you* doing?"

"I thought we were watching airplanes!"

Emily was dumbstruck. "You *really* came here to watch airplanes just to be with me?"

"Yeah. What did you think was gonna happen?"

Emily was simultaneously embarrassed and impressed. She crawled off Fred, and they had a long talk about dating, making out, and the fact that Fred really did just want to be with her to get to know her. In contrast to her past boyfriends, he wasn't interested in just her body.

Emily says, "That third date was hilarious, in hindsight, but a good picture of Fred's integrity. It also highlighted the difference in where both of us were coming from."

The challenge they've faced as a married couple is a difference in libido. Fred's is lower than Emily's. "I'm good to go almost anytime," Emily confesses. "And if he wants to do it multiple times in the same day, I'm all for it!"

For their honeymoon, they traveled to Florida. Emily expected they'd have a sexual free-for-all, with sex happening a couple times a day, every day.

Fred had different plans. "We were paying a lot of money to be there, and we had tickets to Disney World, which aren't cheap. I expected us to get out of the hotel room every now and then."

Almost immediately, Emily took Fred's lesser concern for sex personally. Even though Fred was happy to have sex two or three times a week, since Emily wanted it every day or even a couple times a day, his "lack of interest" made her think she was no longer attractive to him. The fact that she had gained almost forty pounds since their engagement made her especially sensitive to her appearance.

Fred also had some unrealistic expectations. "I found sex to be a lot of work. Helping Emily reach orgasm wasn't easy."

As a pastor, I gently inquired about what I found out to be true—both Fred and Emily had a history with porn, and in porn, women easily orgasm during intercourse. In real life, wives orgasming during intercourse alone is actually not very common. Dr. Maureen Whelihan, an obstetrician and gynecologist and an expert with the American College of Obstetricians and Gynecologists, says between 70 percent to 90 percent of women are unable to achieve orgasm with penetration alone (absent clitoral stimulation).[37] Porn actresses are just that—*actresses*. Fred also discovered that Emily required another "ten minutes or so" of stimulation beyond intercourse, which isn't uncommon either; in fact, it's actually much less than most wives require. But Fred didn't know that, and it took some of the fun out of their sexual encounters.

This is yet another example of the disinformation an entire

generation of spouses is facing because of porn. Satan and his servants *lie* (see John 8:44). If you're struggling in the bedroom, begin with these questions: Are my expectations of what sex is supposed to be like realistic, or are they born from misinformation? Are we supposed to sexually desire each other seven days a week? Do most couples frequently get so hot and bothered that the clothes come off at the mere thought of being intimate? Is every sexual encounter in marriage supposed to be better and more intense than the last one? Is sex not supposed to take a little work and a lot of communication to grow and flourish—just like every other area of marriage does?

I see far too many couples resent the fact that sex isn't always easy, and I want to ask them, "Who told you that it is?"

The frustration Emily and Fred faced in the bedroom meant Fred wanted sex less and less, but Emily's level of desire hadn't changed at all. "Emily's pursuit of me sexually was a constant; she'd slip into the shower behind me or come into my office and start unbuttoning my pants."

Emily concurs. "He's not wrong. I was after him every day, or even later in the day if we'd had sex in the morning." His lack of reciprocation frustrated and hurt her. She'd tell him, "Do you have any idea how many husbands wish their wives were like me?"

Fred knew that was true, but he insisted, "You don't give me a chance to be the pursuer."

DIFFERENT DRIVES

Every spouse has the right to say no. Sex isn't a handshake. It takes a significant amount of relational, emotional, and physical energy, and sometimes one or both partners just can't get there.

Excessive pouting or resentment over a refusal that makes the other spouse "give in" can be manipulative and coercive. It's almost always best to focus on creating a sexual relationship marked by mutual pleasure, with each partner's spiritual, emotional, relational, and physical health (all of which can interfere with libido) addressed. In many marriages, when those issues are addressed, the sexual frustrations will disappear as well.

The challenge is to learn how to communicate hurt and dissatisfaction with what's not happening in the bedroom in a healthy way that increases understanding and empathy. Pouting doesn't help, but gritting your teeth to simmer in silent resentment doesn't help either. There has to be a third way.

The sense of alienation and anger that can arise when different libidos collide is due in part to the fact that we reserve sexual intimacy for marriage. Therefore, anything we deny our spouse becomes an absolute denial. Our spouse can have other needs met by other people and friendships, but not their sexual needs. *Needs* may seem too strong a word, since no one will die from a lack of sex, but if you're not facing abuse or relational breakdown, excusing the fact that you're willing to let your spouse wallow in misery as long as they're not *dying* is a precarious perch from which to build a satisfying marriage. When a wife or husband feels they are left hanging sexually, it can feel like *emotional* abandonment and not just sexual abandonment.

Learning to navigate this challenge, however, can do wonders for a marriage. The skills we develop to understand and serve each other when we are intimate can benefit the marriage in every facet of married life.

A relatively recent distinction that has helped a lot of couples is the difference between "spontaneous drive" and "responsive drive." *Spontaneous* drive is the drive of someone who doesn't need much of a trigger to desire sex. They live on the edge of sexual excitement, so a flash of their spouse's body or a suggestive touch can make them ready to go. They're "primed" for sex most of the time and don't need a trigger to think sex will be enjoyable. Emily is, of course, a "spontaneous drive" spouse.

Responsive drive is the drive of someone who doesn't really desire sex until they allow themselves to be sexually stimulated. In other words, they often don't want sex until they start having sex. Their brain operates in such a way that they need some form of desired physical caressing before the thought of sex seems appealing. If they don't allow the touch to start, sex seems more like a chore than a welcome invitation. Once sex happens, they may be thoroughly satisfied, but because of the way their brain works, they tend to love *memories* of sex more than the *anticipation* of sex. If sex never seems like a particularly exciting option for you, but after a session of sexual intimacy, you think, *Why don't we do this more often?* you may be a "responsive drive" spouse.

Your sex drive is not a fault or a problem; your brain is what it is. But understanding the difference between spontaneous drive and responsive drive can do wonders for addressing the frustrations that sometimes arise due to differing libidos. If you're a responsive drive spouse, it helps to remember that just because you don't often desire sex doesn't mean your relationship wouldn't benefit from more frequent sexual intimacy. You may be married to someone with a spontaneous drive. Regardless, communication with and a good understanding of your spouse are key.

MATTHEW AND COURTNEY: A HIGHER-DRIVE HUSBAND

Matthew and Courtney sought to understand this dynamic when it became apparent that Matthew has a much higher drive than Courtney does. They are committed to their marriage and were happy with so much about their relationship, but the tension in the bedroom led them to study and apply this information about different drives. Matthew began reading numerous books and blogs in an effort to understand how their differing drives could be addressed. He recognized that some of the breakdown was due to his lack of communication skills. He was telling Courtney *what* he wanted, but not *why* he wanted it. For him, it wasn't just about sexual release. Focusing only on whether they would have sex didn't create relational understanding; it just led to an impasse. And the way he was responding to her refusals wasn't helping either.

After Matthew started to better communicate what was really going on, Courtney began to do some research as well, which led her to realize she is a "responsive drive" spouse. "Matthew is a generous lover. He never leaves me unsatisfied—so why didn't I want to have sex more often? The 'responsive drive' explanation made sense to me."

Recognizing the way her brain works, she started trying to be more open to Matthew's advances. Instead of always defaulting to no or shaming him for wanting to have sex on a regular basis, she at least allowed the advances to have the potential to turn into having sex.

Before, when Matthew started to rub Courtney's back in bed and she was viewing it as a sexual invitation, she'd tense up and say, "Not tonight," or "I have a headache," or "I have to wake up early." She explains, "Once I even said, 'But we just had sex'—even though it had been two weeks."

Now Courtney spoke kindly but firmly to herself. *It's okay, he's just massaging you. Relax, don't say an automatic no, see if you can get into this, and accept that this is his way of showing love. You can show you love him by touching him back.*

The initial months of their sexual reawakening were, in Courtney's words, "a roller coaster," but in time, as things gradually improved, Courtney became even more committed to growing their sexual intimacy because she saw how it improved all aspects of their marriage and made Matthew feel much closer to her.

"It's not just the thirty or so minutes sex takes; it's the thirty or so hours afterward that sets a whole new tone in the relationship," Courtney reflects. "I certainly enjoy sex, but I enjoy the relationship following sex just as much."

PERSPECTIVE

If differing libido levels have been an issue in your marriage, it helps to gain a little perspective. Though a difference in libidos is often talked about as a problem, in reality it's the norm for almost every couple. It should be obvious, but this is one of those crazy expectations we never think to challenge, even though *very few couples have exactly the same level of libido.* It's unusual when both spouses want sex the same amount of time or always at the same time. We need to stop talking as if there's something "wrong" with a marriage that mirrors the life experience of the vast majority of couples!

And why make this difference sound so much more important than other differences? Most couples diverge when it comes to the timing of other aspects of their relationship—serious conversations, playful outings, or eating out. There are a lot of areas where desires don't match in marriage. Expecting to overcome different libidos by trying to make them the same isn't true to life. We can be gentle and understanding with our spouse, but we can't change them.

Jessa Zimmerman, a certified sex therapist from Seattle, says that the challenge is multiplied when the higher-libido spouse "takes the partner's lower desire personally so they feel unloved." Making your partner's level of desire about you, Zimmerman says, "is pretty misguided because someone's desire is inherent to them and how they work; it's not really about your partner." In fact, taking it personally not only does great damage to the marriage (as we saw with Emily and Fred), but it can "change the meaning of the sex you're having. Now your partner has to show up to have sex for you to feel good about yourself."[38] Instead of a way to mutually enjoy each other, sex becomes a test of a person's worth.

The other danger Zimmerman points out is that the lower-desire spouse can start to feel broken, as if something is wrong with them. Fred's desire was entirely appropriate for him; nothing was wrong with him. This can go both ways, of course. At times, Emily wondered if there was something wrong with *her* since she seemed to desire sex more than most wives, especially when she kept hearing about how husbands are supposed to be the ones constantly chasing down their wives.

Pressuring your spouse, making them feel guilty or broken, is abuse. It perpetuates and even exacerbates the divide. We're called to cherish our spouse, even as we invite them into a deeper, more intimate connection. Everyone has their own unique "desire potential," so focus on helping your spouse achieve their highest pleasure through an increased understanding of how their brain operates. If you're the higher-drive spouse, you will benefit immensely from doing your own personal work so you don't make your spouse's response a statement of your own worth. If a husband or wife doesn't like to cook, that doesn't mean they don't care about their spouse being hungry. They just may not naturally treasure the process that makes them not hungry!

Zimmerman urges spouses with the lower libido to "create a whole lot of maybe." This is a two-person effort. The higher-libido spouse has to be open to "maybe" and not take it personally. The lower-desire spouse has to generously but honestly say, "Well, I may not be in the mood, but let's start and see what happens." Starting is not a guarantee that there will be an ending. But you can kiss a little and cuddle and see if something is awakened. Much of the time, sexual desire *will* show up, but it won't 100 percent of the time, and both partners need to be okay with that. Everyone has the right to say no, even after you've started.

The important thing is to view sexual play as an outing rather than as a specific act. Zimmerman likens it to a playground. When you agree to go to a playground, you may not go down the slide. You may stop at the swing. But you don't call it a failure if you stay on the swing. The outing was successful because you were together, enjoyed yourselves, and experienced a certain level of intimacy. One wife knew her husband just didn't have the energy at the end of a long day to have intercourse, but she asked him, "Can we just hold each other while we're naked?" She wanted to connect on a level that seemed realistic, and her husband agreed. There's neuroscience behind this wife's request, by the way.

Hugging releases a good bit of oxytocin, the "cuddle chemical" in our brains that makes us feel close. It doesn't release quite as much as an orgasm does, but it's still significant.

STRESS UPON STRESS

Let's go back to Emily and Fred and see how they found some resolution with a higher-drive wife. Emily and Fred's reversal began with a spiritual movement in Emily's life. "This is where you come in," Emily told me. "I got a copy of *Sacred Marriage*. From the very start, when you wrote about God designing marriage to make us holy more than happy, I could sense that God was telling me, *You have been living for what you want and have missed focusing on your husband, including seeing the ways he loves you other than wanting to have sex as often as you do.*"

Emily remembers, "Finishing that book was a huge wake-up call for me."

She purchased a picture frame, set it next to Fred's sink in the master bathroom, and used dry-erase markers to write daily encouragements. Every day she wrote something new:

"I love you because you made me pancakes."
"I love you for changing the oil in my car."
"I love you for changing the baby's diaper and getting up
    with her last night when she was crying."
"I love you for being an insanely funny dad with our
    children."
Sometimes the message was a little provocative: "I love the
    way your butt looks in the pants you're wearing today."

The daily dry-erase board comments were revolutionary for both Emily and Fred. Emily says, "It changed me. [She started crying as she remembered this.] It changed my focus from my disappointment about him not pursuing me sexually to all the amazing ways he was loving me that I had been missing because I was so focused on that one area."

For Fred, it was a huge hit of motivation. "I so appreciated that she was seeing those things and everything I was trying to do to show her I love her, and that made me want to do even more of that for her."

If there is a frustration in any area of your marriage, please consider embracing the art of encouraging. Don't let your marriage become defined by one disappointment. Push back with many expressions of gratitude. What does your spouse do that delights you? Write it out. Speak it. Thank God for it. That's Philippians 4:8 in action.

Fred lived with a new joy. "Emily's attitude toward me changed. It was less of a constant expectation for sex that I could never live up to, and more about her just loving me as a husband with it not having to be about sex all the time. That was more appealing to me. I love her as my wife, not just as my sex partner."

Emily adds, "I didn't write those things on the board to get him to do more. I just wanted him to know, 'I see you.'"

PERSONAL WORK

After gaining perspective on their different libidos, both Fred and Emily needed to do some personal work. Both of them completely swore off any use of porn, and Emily needed to undertake some trauma work. She had faced deep trauma as a young girl and finally sought counseling to deal with the ensuing anxiety and depression. She and Fred started out in marital counseling, but a wise counselor explained that since it was clear to him that Emily had PTSD, they needed to treat that first before they could address the marital issues.

"I went through eighteen months of EMDR therapy, and I can't say enough about how hard and how necessary that was for me and for Fred."[39]

"Emily's therapy work, as difficult as it was, created a massive change in our relationship," Fred says. "Her attitude was pleasant and lovely, and her personality lit up in ways I had never seen before."

She also underwent a necessary surgery and refocused on her overall physical health, which, as Fred observed, "created another huge leap in her energy and vibrancy."

Emily's decision to deal with her codependency issues was another component of their healing. She told her therapist, "I feel like I'm always chasing Fred."

"Why do you think you do that?"

"I don't know, but it's terrifying."

"What makes it terrifying?"

"Because he might not chase me back."

Emily came to understand that "Fred *was* pursuing me, but I wasn't seeing it. I equated sexual pursuit with personal pursuit, and they're not the same." Sex can serve your relationship, but it should never define your relationship.

All of this is a good reminder that sexual issues are almost never solely about sex. Spiritual healing (getting rid of porn), emotional healing (dealing with trauma), physical healing (poor health can seriously inhibit sexual desire and performance), and relational healing (anger and bitterness are libido assassins) are all important areas that may need attention.*

EMILY AND FRED TODAY

Emily is still up for sex just about any day. "What can I say? Fred's a very pretty man, and he's getting even prettier as he gets older. I'm forty-five and at the peak of my libido, so anytime he's ready, I'm willing."

What about Fred? "I still like doing other things," he says with a laugh.

"Sometimes he'd rather go hiking!" Emily adds. "Can you believe it?"

But they've settled into having sex just about every other day, and both of them seem content with that.

"We occasionally have 'twofer Thursdays' or 'multiple Mondays,' and then even Emily might want to take a couple days off," says Fred with a twinkle in his eye.

The key is that both of them are happy with where they are. Emily could desire sex more than three or four times a week, but she's content with what she's getting. And Fred probably wouldn't choose four times a week on his own, but he delights in pleasing Emily. Their differing libidos were once a source of great pain and heartache, but they've found a way to make them a source of joy and comfort.

When it comes to divergent libidos, there's no right or wrong answer to how often a couple "should" have sex. I'm more concerned

---

* Debra Fileta and I address these issues more thoroughly in our book *Married Sex*.

that each partner feels valued, adored, cherished, and desired. The key is that sex becomes a blessing to the marriage rather than a burden. That's how you make your marriage a fortress.

A COMMITMENT TO CONTENTMENT

Matthew and Courtney also remain committed to mutually enjoyable intimacy. "I know Courtney is willing to be aroused," Matthew says, "If I can't do that, we don't have sex. I'm not interested in having sex with someone who doesn't want to have sex with me."

So on nights when Courtney just can't get there, Matthew can tell, and he'll often be the first to say, "Let's just go to sleep."

"Are you sure?" Courtney will ask, admitting that she feels bad for him when that happens.

The biggest change in their marriage is their empathy for each other. That's what makes their marriage a fortress. Sometimes Courtney's love for Matthew means being open to intimacy when she initially isn't into it. And sometimes Matthew's love for Courtney means not pushing for sex when she just can't desire it like he does. Neither Courtney nor Matthew can *change* their brains—and they shouldn't have to—but they can *manage* their brains. Courtney can have empathy for Matthew, and Matthew can have empathy for Courtney.

From a "lunar schedule" (once a month) they've settled into a fairly regular two to three times a week. Matthew is satisfied with this but admits, "More would be good. I'd like to have sex four or five times a week, but it's not worth the trade-off to have Courtney feel overwhelmed."

If he were to pout about the fact that he wasn't getting sex four or five times a week, he'd wreck the two or three times a week that they do have sex. His pouting wouldn't be an attitude that fostered empathy or intimacy. But if Courtney expected him to be content with once a month, she wouldn't be showing empathy or fostering understanding either.

I appreciate Matthew's attitude. "Our sexual relationship is much better now than it was," he says. "It's not that I'm getting everything I want, but that's life, and I'm satisfied. I also wish I had a higher income than I do, but we have a good life and I need to be content with what's realistic."

When a higher-drive spouse expects that a lower-drive spouse can have sex as often as they would like, without compromise you'll likely end up with two frustrated spouses. Notice that both Emily and Matthew (the two higher-drive spouses) have learned contentment with a little less intimate activity than they would want in their "perfect world," and both Fred and Courtney (the lower-drive spouses) have learned to be open to a little more activity than they would prefer on their own. The writer of Ecclesiastes warns of a man whose "eyes were not content with his wealth" (4:8). Notice the source of discontent: *with his wealth*. "More" isn't always the best answer. Some singles go years without sex. Many spouses lovingly endure months without sex when their spouse is ill or emotionally drained.

Paul tells Timothy that "godliness with contentment is great gain . . . But if we have food and clothing, we will be content with that" (1 Timothy 6:6, 8). Sex isn't on that list!

Having said that, it's not healthy, spiritually or relationally, for either spouse to feel like a martyr—one because they must suffer what feels like a sexless marriage; and the other because they feel like they must give in and have sex when they don't necessarily desire it. As I said at the beginning of this chapter, I'm not speaking about marriages where abuse or relational breakdown are making sexual relations unwelcomed and unwise. The teaching here is for emotionally attached marriages where one spouse is seeking empathy (for their frustration) and the other is seeking understanding (for their level of desire, whether high or low). Spiritual health is best served by *both* spouses growing in character, maturity, and intimacy—not pointing fingers, not making unrealistic demands, but both searching their own hearts for what's really going on.

When I do premarital counseling, I ask the couples to memorize James 4:1–3:

> What causes fights and quarrels among you? Don't they come from your desires that battle within you? You desire but do not have, so you kill. You covet but you cannot get what you want, so you quarrel and fight. You do not have because you do not ask God. When you ask, you do not receive, because you ask with wrong motives, that you may spend what you get on your pleasures.

This passage has taught me to first search my own heart before I bring something up with my wife. I know what I want, but what are my motives for wanting it? Most often, I see selfishness on my part, and I need to repent rather than put this load on my wife. Far less often, there may be selfishness on my wife's part, and as her brother in Christ I can humbly bring it up, open to the fact that I may be wrong, and ask her to search her heart before God if I'm not.

It's easy to assume it might be selfish to want more sex. But it's not wrong to desire more sex—your brain is what it is—and it's not wrong to let your spouse know of your desires. Demanding, coercing, and pouting are abusive. But courageous, vulnerable confession in a spirit of contentment is lovely. It's a call to greater intimacy, empathy, and understanding.

If after this courageous confession you still don't get what you want and you begin to obsess over the gap between what you have and what you want in your "perfect" world, you'll assault your own happiness and spiritual well-being. Paul was celibate when he wrote, "I have learned to be content whatever the circumstances" (Philippians 4:11). I'm not asking any woman or man in an otherwise healthy marriage to simply put up with a sexless or near sexless marriage. I'm just asking them to address the situation in a loving way as they seek understanding and then counsel if there is an impasse. The goal is for both spouses to grow in character, spiritual maturity, understanding, and empathy and thus to become more connected by addressing their differing libidos rather than allowing unaddressed differences to alienate them from each other. Learn how different desires for the *quantity* of sex can create an increased desire for a more connected and higher *quality* of marriage and result in both spouses feeling cherished, valued, listened to, and understood.

LESSONS LEARNED

Matthew and Courtney have made their marriage a fortress against differing sexual drives by learning to unleash a much higher level of communication. That's probably the biggest change in Matthew's life. "We communicate better *and* faster."

They talk about what's going on in each other's brains rather than silently resenting one's desires and the other's refusals. This points to a major marital principle that is essential for deep intimacy: conflict in any area should lead to *deeper understanding*. Keep pressing forward so that you understand your spouse more and resent him or her less.

Matthew urges husbands, "If you're frustrated about your sex life, don't just focus on sex. Most often, the underlying problems are communication and attitude." Talk to each other, listen to each other, and be devoted to *serving* each other. Selfishness that always demands and selfishness that always refuses are *both* ugly.* If your spouse isn't happy, that's a problem. Ignoring their happiness or refusing to care about it is as harmful to your relationship as failing to stop a bleeding wound is to your body. You'll bleed out.

"Courtney and I used to point fingers a lot, so that's why we stress better communication. Too many couples focus on the sex but don't explain to each other why they want sex or don't want sex, so they never reach a place of understanding."

Explaining the "why" behind desiring sex or not desiring sex can be a game changer. When Emily wants Fred to know she treasures the bonding and safety that follow intimacy, and when Matthew explains that he never feels closer to Courtney than after sharing a sexual experience, it becomes more of a relational issue than a personal issue. It's not just "What do *I* want?" but rather "What do *we* need?"

When Fred explains that he wants to do something fun outside the bedroom because he enjoys Emily's friendship, and when Courtney explains that she really does enjoy sex with Matthew but

---

* Again, it's not selfish to refuse sex in the case of abuse or addictions that have led to betrayal trauma.

it can take a while for her brain to kick into gear, it's easier for Emily and Matthew not to take the differing libidos so personally. And remember that couples often forget what they've already discussed. "Understanding" is dynamic, not static. Intimacy is best served when we patiently keep talking about what's going on inside us, as it simply takes time for us to rewire our brains, stop judging, and replace our condemnation of each other with a new understanding.

Matthew has a particular concern that, in cases where the wife has a lower drive, the wives understand that "husbands don't just want their wives' bodies. They want to feel connected to you and loved by you. It's not *just* physical."

Remembering his own journey, Matthew also urges the higher-drive spouse to "focus on *progress*, not *perfection*. If we focus on what's still not perfect, we'll miss how much progress has been made."

Courtney believes the effort she is putting into their sexual relationship has been more than worth it. "I'm much happier in my marriage. The weight of those ill feelings and resentment and guardedness has lifted. It feels *so* much better." Plus, she really enjoys having sex more often. Matthew has gone out of his way to be creative and to make it more fun and pleasurable, which in turn helps her to look forward to intimacy more often.

So for the higher-drive spouse, remember that you have work to do as well. Try to make each sexual encounter as pleasurable for your spouse as you can. They should never feel used, but rather pleasured, served, and cherished.

And for the lower-drive spouse? Courtney counsels, "One of the biggest things I tell the lower-drive spouse is to try to see things from your spouse's perspective. Put yourself in their shoes."

Courtney feels safe in saying this because she knows she is

married to a man who cares about her pleasure and well-being. Out of that secure place, she's willing to be appropriately challenged, which has resulted in a pretty nice payoff. "I like having sex more often," Courtney says. "With more frequent sex, trust and happiness have grown, and I see my husband with a clearer vision. I understand him better." She thought she was having sex more often to please her husband; in the end, she believes it has served her even more.

To those men and women who are married to "responsive drive" partners, Matthew counsels that "the hardest part is going to be that you may constantly feel you are not desired. But you need to realize that just because your spouse isn't initiating sex doesn't mean they don't like you or that they don't like to have sex with you. They just have a different brain. You can't fault them for what they want or don't want. Try not to take it personally." Wisely counseling the higher-drive spouse not to become coercive or demanding, Matthew adds, "Don't fight about whether your spouse initiates. They often can't help it. Just be glad they're willing to be responsive."

Matthew explains, "If Courtney isn't aroused, I don't expect her to crawl all over me, but if I *can* get her aroused, I'll feel like the sexiest man on earth!" Rather than feeling frustrated that she wasn't excited, he's proud to have been able to get her there. That sounds like a much healthier place to live.

It's difficult to make your marriage a fortress if one of the relationship's primary building blocks—sexual intimacy—is tearing you apart rather than bonding you more closely. Living with a subpar sexual relationship puts your marriage at risk. Learning how to understand, please, serve, and have compassion for each other will turn your marriage into a fortress.

Building Your Fortress Takeaways

1. Enjoyable sex can't save a bad marriage, but bad sex can certainly keep a marriage from feeling good.
2. The teaching in this chapter and the takeaways are not intended for marriages in which abuse or addiction is present. In those cases, talking about the frequency of marital relations can cause more harm.
3. If you're struggling in the bedroom, begin with this question: Are my expectations of what sex is supposed to be like realistic, or are they born out of misinformation?
4. Every spouse should have the right to say, "Not tonight," without fear of reprisal. When libidos collide, it's best to focus on creating a sexual relationship marked by mutual pleasure, with each partner's spiritual, emotional, relational, and physical health (all of which can interfere with libido) addressed.
5. The sense of alienation and anger that can arise when differing libidos collide may be due, at least in part, to the fact that sexual intimacy is reserved for marriage, so anything we deny our spouse becomes an absolute denial. Sexual intimacy is one of the few experiences in life a marriage offers that no other relationship or person can.
6. When a wife or husband is left hanging sexually, it sometimes feels like emotional abandonment, not just sexual abandonment.

7. The skills we develop to understand and serve each other during physical intimacy will benefit every facet of marriage, helping to create a more intimate union.

8. Understanding the difference between spontaneous drive and responsive drive can do wonders for addressing differing libidos in a healthy way.

9. Expecting your spouse to desire sex as much or as little as you do isn't true to life. No doubt you and your spouse have many conflicting desires that have nothing to do with sex. You can't fix a difference in libidos; instead, learn to manage it in a way that builds emotional connection instead of causing marital drift.

10. *Maybe* (rather than an automatic *yes* or *no*) can be a helpful word when one spouse desires sex and the other isn't sure yet. You always maintain the right to say no if you need to.

11. Higher-libido spouses can decrease their own frustration by not taking their spouse's lower desire personally or making it about them.

12. Guard against either spouse feeling "broken" for having a different sex drive. Remember that your brain is what it is.

13. Sexual issues are almost never solely about sex. There may need to be spiritual, emotional, or physical healing on an individual basis before a couple's sexual issues can be addressed.

14. Ideally, neither spouse will feel like they are being a martyr, always giving in or always being shut down. This feeling can lead to alienation.

15. It's not wrong to desire more sex or to let your spouse know of your desire. "Courageous confession" is a healthy approach; demands and coercion are abusive. If you refuse to be content with compromise and obsess over the gap between what you have and what you want in your "perfect" world, you risk bringing much stress to your marriage.

16. Try to use conflict to increase understanding rather than letting it pull you apart. Keep pressing forward so that you understand your spouse more and resent them less.

17. Explaining the "why" behind desiring sex or not desiring sex can make a dramatic difference and lead to greater understanding and attachment.

• • • • • • • • • • • • •

CHAPTER 7

FAITH AND FINANCES

Using Money to Draw You Closer Instead of Pulling You Apart

Donna looked at the menu and fought back tears when she saw the prices.

She wasn't at a Michelin three-star restaurant. She wasn't at a Michelin one-star restaurant. She wasn't even at Ruth's Criss Steak House. She was at Outback.*

Donna was with her kids, reading the menu from right to left (price first) and wondering if she should share a kids' meal with her young son. Would her extended family notice? Would they find out just how bad things were financially for her and her husband?

"I wanted to curl up in a ball and cry. I wanted to leave the restaurant, even though I was really hungry, because I was exhausted from trying to make things work financially."

---

* In the United States, Outback Steakhouse is a casual dining restaurant chain catering to budget-minded patrons.

In the end, Donna's dad picked up the check, but she never wanted to feel that vulnerable again.

• • •

Emma walked up to the comfortable-looking suburban home and prayed—literally *prayed*—that no one would answer the doorbell. She was there to sell Avon. One day in the future, she'd have a PhD and be a sought-after education expert. But now she was soaking wet, standing in the rain, hoping she wouldn't have to make a sales pitch but could just leave a catalog behind. Those books got heavy after a while, and Emma had walked a mile and a half to that affluent suburban neighborhood because she and her husband, Billy, could only afford one car and he needed it to get to his construction job.

Emma didn't know it at the time, but she was on quite the ride. Her husband would eventually earn, and then lose, millions of dollars. For a while, she'd live day-to-day, on one occasion even counting coins so she could feed her two boys. But later in life, she'd watch her husband write checks worth tens of thousands of dollars to help families in need. After giving away millions of dollars total, she and Billy would end up having to sell their family home and rent an empty nest house from their son. Their financial roller coaster would take them to heights many couples couldn't even imagine, but also plunge them into terrifying falls that many couples couldn't survive. In the end, this roller coaster would draw them into a deeper intimacy and faith.

• • •

In this chapter, I want to explore how both affluence and financial deprivation can be enhancers rather than destroyers of your relationship. For while these two couples have faced down (and one of them continues to endure) financial deprivation, financial prosperity carries its own marital curses. A CNBC headline from a few years ago, "Being Rich May Increase Your Odds of Divorce" didn't surprise me at all.[40] A highly successful businessman once told me, "Our marriage began falling apart when I went from earning hundreds of thousands of dollars a year to millions of dollars a year."

Divorce statistics are notorious to deconstruct, but news items alone tell us extreme wealth doesn't make your marriage a fortress. Elon Musk, the richest man in the world as I write this, has been divorced twice and just recently semi-separated from an unmarried relationship with a third woman. Bill Gates and Jeff Bezos, numbers two and three of the richest men, are also divorced. Donald Trump's three wives, Larry Ellison's four wives, and Richard Perelman's five wives also show that being a billionaire doesn't guarantee marital bliss.

Finances *impact* a marriage, but they needn't *define* it—either through prosperity or deprivation. Let's look at two couples who have faced want and plenty and see what they've learned.

IGNORANT BLISS

Donna and Kirk were both working when they got married, but they were spending everything that was coming in. Kirk says, "We bought a house, had two car payments, and kept spending our income on stuff with nothing to show for it. We didn't save anything."

When their first baby arrived, Donna quit her job. She had been earning more than Kirk, which meant they went from two incomes to less than half of what they had been making. Donna, an accountant, handled their books but didn't communicate much with Kirk about what was really going on. They went through some job transfers and relocations, and Kirk finally decided he needed to get a handle on their financial situation as they contemplated applying for a new house loan. "I had been living in ignorant bliss. Then I found out we had $40,000 in credit card debt and my income was $35,000 a year. When Donna finally told me how bad it was, I was mad—at Donna and at the debt. How had this happened? Why hadn't she said something? Because she was an accountant, I figured she was finding a way to make things work instead of letting us get so deep into debt."

"He doesn't get mad very often," Donna reflects. "Ninety-eight percent of things don't bother him, but if you step into the 2 percent, you find out."

"I felt a little bit like she had dropped a bomb on me," Kirk explains. "Like, I put my trust in you and you betrayed me. You're an accountant! I had to take a step back and walk away. There wasn't a lot of love between us. It took a couple of days to start talking about it again."

Kirk remembers that the revelation of their debt "felt like getting kicked in the stomach," but eventually he began to see his own role in the mess they were in. "I shouldn't have put that burden solely on her."

Upon reflection, he wasn't just angry with Donna; he was angry with himself too. "Clearly, I wasn't keeping my eye on the ball."

ANGER

This is a good place to correct one of the most misunderstood passages of Scripture: "'In your anger do not sin.' Do not let the sun go down while you are still angry, and do not give the devil a foothold" (Ephesians 4:26–27). Your financial matters may or may not be causing you and your spouse to be angry with each other. But if you fail to deal productively with those issues, you can be assured that your relationship will at some point be negatively affected.

The misunderstanding occurs when the middle statement— "do not let the sun go down while you are still angry"—is removed from the context of the other two phrases: don't let your anger lead you to sin and don't give the devil a foothold. Some couples will take this to mean they shouldn't go to sleep if they're still angry, and so they stay up and keep arguing. As a result, the relationship may suffer more harm.

The apostle Paul is offering general wisdom (the first phrase is from Psalm 4:4, part of Wisdom Literature), not a literal command to be applied legalistically. Paul wants us to know that anger is dangerous and can become a tool used by Satan to pull us apart. This is a warning worth heeding! The bit about "do not let the sun go down" (which many people tend to focus on) is based on several accounts from Deuteronomy that tie a particular action to the sunset, as commentator Markus Barth notes: "The sunset is the time limit for several actions: goods taken as a pawn from a poor man have to be returned, a hired hand's wages have to be paid out, the body of a man who has been impaled must be buried."[41]

The principle is this: Don't delay what should be done. If you wait until tomorrow to pay someone who needs and deserves the money today, you sin against that person, even though you are paying them. In Ephesians 4:26–27, Paul is underscoring the danger of living with unresolved or unreconciled anger. These are wise words for any marriage to apply.

Anger is a normal emotion in life and marriage, and its expression is not always sinful. Moses was angry when he broke the tablets containing the Ten Commandments, even *sharing* God's anger. But when in his anger he struck the rock to bring out water, God called him out on it. The outburst that followed that anger *wasn't* okay.[42]

N. T. Wright's take is helpful here: "It simply won't do to go with the flow of whatever you happen to feel at the time . . . We should regard our moods, and the speech which flows from them, as we might a strong but wilful horse, which needs to be reminded frequently of the direction we're supposed to be going in."[43]

In your marriage, if an issue comes up at 11:00 p.m. and you're both tired and talking it out seems to be making things worse, you are not disobeying Ephesians 4:26 by getting a good night's sleep and eating a bagel for breakfast before you gather your thoughts to have a constructive conversation. In fact, Kirk needed to let his anger sit for *a couple of days* before he could have a healthy talk with Donna about what had happened. He needed to cool off and process. He was doing what Paul said: refusing to let his anger be a foothold for Satan. Had he simply let the matter drop and never come back to talk about it, that would have been giving Satan a foothold. At the same time, speaking while enraged could have done the same thing. Remember, Ephesians 4:26 has *three* principles, not one:

1. Don't let your anger lead you to sin.
2. Don't unnecessarily delay getting rid of your anger.

3. Don't let your anger become a foothold that Satan can use to ruin your relationship.

Paul's use of the sunset imagery ("do not let the sun go down") is a creative way—familiar to any Jew who had read Deuteronomy (Ephesus had a significant Jewish population)—to say, "Bring this urgent matter to a necessary and timely resolution." In my anecdotal experience as a pastor, much harm has been done when people read Ephesians 4:26 and separate the "sunset" clause from the general points Paul is making and thus keep arguing into the early hours of the morning, making each other miserable and growing further apart.

Now back to the finances.

GETTING THE SHIP SAILING AGAIN

It was a mature and wise decision on Kirk's part to pause, sort out his anger, study it, pray about it, and use it for self-reflection—and *then* to talk to Donna about their situation. Kirk was doing exactly what Paul urged in Ephesians 4:26, even though it wasn't within a twenty-four-hour time frame.

Donna also admitted her part. "We should have both been involved in handling the debt. I would tell all couples you *both* need to be involved in what's happening financially, even if one of you is a professional accountant."

Dr. Siang-Yang Tan is a friend of mine. His wife is an accountant. While talking together at a conference, we were laughing about how our wives control our finances to the point that neither of us feels confident about how to write a check. (With so much of banking online these days, it would take me a good hour and the unearthing of a couple of passwords to pay a single bill.) Dr. Tan's wife has been such a good steward that he faced his recent retirement from Fuller Seminary and as a longtime senior pastor without concern. It's not unusual for one spouse to control the finances, but the difference is that Dr. Tan has a general picture of their financial situation.

I do the same with Lisa. About four times a year, she shows me what we have in savings and investments. If cash flow is an issue, she'll tell me what we need to meet our obligations. And in the last quarter of each year, we're always evaluating what we've earned and what we've given.

Kirk and Donna's situation became perilous, not because Donna handled the finances, but because not enough communication was happening for them to avoid intimacy-busting conflict. Once Kirk became aware of the fact that they owed more money than they earned in a year, he and Donna sat down and wrote down all their expenses. Donna started reading books on personal finance. They sold one of their cars and stopped eating out.

"You'd be amazed at how much you can spend without having anything to show for it," Donna says. They didn't buy Christmas presents for each other that first year—just for the kids—and then started transferring credit card debt to cards with 0 percent interest for eighteen months and no transfer fees. (Note that it's more difficult, if not impossible, to do that nowadays.) They also followed the Dave Ramsey "debt snowball" model and slowly began to climb out of debt.[*]

---

[*] The debt snowball method involves paying off the smallest debt first and then taking the money that had been allocated to that debt and rolling it on to the next smallest one.

Lack of communication about their financial situation had led to anger and distance, but facing and then overcoming the challenge together helped build a *new* level of intimacy. "It opened us up to more communication," says Kirk. They couldn't do many of the fun things they used to do because they didn't have the money, but talking about how to get out of debt became a shared passion.

Though they were still in debt, Donna and Kirk began to tithe, something they had never done before. They did this out of their love for the Lord, not because they thought doing so would obligate God to bless them back. Even so, just months later, Kirk got a substantial raise, and within three years his income doubled from their rock-bottom moment. In less than four years, they paid off the last of their credit cards and were debt-free except for their mortgage.

Donna will never forget that day. She told Kirk, "I just paid off our final credit card. We're completely debt-free. Let's go celebrate."

They lit all the paid-off credit cards on fire and then went out to eat at Outback, paying the tab with cash. Donna ordered the filet mignon.

EXPECTATIONS

Emma and Billy's story doesn't wrap up nearly so neatly. They met in school when they were just twelve years old because their last names put them sitting side by side. Though they went to the same private middle school and high school together, they didn't have their first date until February of their senior year.

Following high school, Billy went to study to become a

missionary aviator, while Emma went on to study pre-med. Emma soon grew weary of trying to keep a long-distance relationship alive, so they decided to find a mutual school they could transfer to, getting engaged the next year, and getting married the year after that (before they graduated).

It wasn't easy. "Our first budget was $972 a month, but the problem was, our combined income was just $436 a month," says Emma.

While going to school, Emma sold Avon and Billy worked construction, though both aspired to pursue much different vocations (they would both eventually get masters and doctorates).

> Finances weren't a strain on our relationship because in our twenties, we didn't know any better. We knew getting married so early would be tough financially, but we preferred being together. If we had come from wealthy families or had it easy, financially speaking, in the early part of our marriage, I don't think we would have the same grit and perseverance that the Lord has built in us. The early challenge helped forge something in us so we could handle the later inevitable struggles.

What strikes me about Emma and Billy is how their realistic expectations saved them from much misery. They knew the first decade was going to be tight financially, so they didn't resent it or feel sorry for themselves. Some young couples expect to live as their parents do now, not as their parents did then (before they were born). They view a budget as oppressive and cruel—as a curse.

If you feel oppressed and cursed, you're not going to be very happy in your marriage. Personal contentment is the necessary foundation of marital satisfaction.

One of the things that gave Emma such a healthy outlook was teaching in an überwealthy community in Southern California. "I had taught in poverty-stricken communities and in a community where some of the kids came to school in a limousine. And you know what I found? Wealthy families weren't any happier. They just had different kinds of problems."

Emma looks back and sees the benefit of her early jobs, even though they felt a bit demeaning at the time. "I was very young and very shy. Going door-to-door and then later working as a receptionist who had to greet people helped me communicate much better as a teacher."

Her outlook is extraordinary. Rather than resenting carrying a heavy load of sales books on foot in the rain to make her Avon pitch, she stresses how much more enjoyable the trip home was "because the bag was a whole lot lighter!" And she treasures how those early challenges set her up to succeed in later positions.

You may be going through a very difficult season. Your attitude will make life sweet or bitter. When Paul told Timothy that "godliness with contentment is great gain" (1 Timothy 6:6), it strikes me that he never once said "financial security is great gain." Biblically, financial security is viewed more as a temptation (see Ecclesiastes 5:10; Matthew 19:23; Luke 12:15; 1 Timothy 6:10), but isn't that a temptation most of us want? Pause for a moment and ask yourself honestly, *What do I value more—contentment or affluence?* You may be tempted to think, *I'd be content if I had affluence,* but that's exactly what Emma discovered was *not* true of the wealthy families whose kids she taught.

Biblical values are clear, though often foreign to the modern mind: character is more important than wealth (Proverbs 22:1), and surrender is the essence of the Christian faith, the kind of trust that believes in God's goodness and yields to his providential care, even if we think life (and therefore God) isn't fair. If God values our character more than our comfort and our faith more than our affluence, it is good of him to use earthly desires to help us inherit heavenly riches. When you pay a barista four bucks for a cup of coffee, for a split second you are four dollars poorer without a cup of coffee in your hand. But you trust that handing over the four bucks will lead to something greater—that vaunted caffeine boost—so you make the exchange. The interval is too short to even be noticed.

From the viewpoint of eternity, handing over earthly riches to receive heavenly glory will eventually feel the same way. Ten thousand years from now, even a few decades of financial frustration will feel like the time it took for a barista to hand over a cappuccino or Americano, and you'll think, *All in all, it was more than worth it.*

In Emma and Billy's case, financial deprivation awakened and strengthened their faith, even when times grew desperate. "There was one Sunday where we had no money, no baby food, and, even worse, no more diapers," says Emma.

At four in the afternoon, there was a knock on their door. "Our Sunday school class collected $400 that morning and sent someone to hand us the cash. Four hundred dollars back then would probably be a couple thousand bucks today. It changed our life. After the couple handed over the money, we said thank you, looked inside the envelope, fell on the floor, and cried."

What were you doing on the nearest Sunday a year ago from the day you're reading this? Few of us remember. Billy and Emma will *never* forget *that* Sunday, which happened decades ago. And that Sunday wouldn't be memorable if they hadn't been so desperate.

REGRETS

Looking back, it's a bit ironic that Emma and Billy may have more regrets about their affluence than they do their financial deprivation. After both earned advanced degrees and started working, they began making millions. Emma was able to focus on education and not go door-to-door selling cosmetics. They bought their first house and started taking vacations.

"We were making so much more than we could have ever imagined or needed," says Emma, but they didn't increase their standard of living so much as they increased their pattern of giving. Both Emma and Billy are givers, so when Billy told Emma, "Let's support these people and that ministry and that work of God," Emma wrote the checks. They were able to provide the full salaries of several missionaries and even sent some of the missionaries' children to college.

Billy always believed you can't outgive God, so he didn't pay much attention to their bottom line and lack of savings and investments, something he now regrets. "Emma took care of the accounting and bookkeeping, but I directed our giving. We weren't gambling or doing drugs, but we gave beyond what, in hindsight, we should have. I didn't worry about saving or investing because I thought I had my entire life ahead of me to save, and I couldn't imagine that the money would stop flowing."

Notice what caused the tension in both Kirk and Donna's and Emma and Billy's marriages: a disconnect in communication about their financial bottom line. If both of you don't have a general idea of your net worth (or debt burden), that's the place to start. It should be shared. Steve Wilke, a coauthor of one of my books,[44] insists that premarital couples run a credit report and give it to each other.

"When you marry someone, you're marrying their credit report as well as the person," he explains. That's part of becoming one.

THE CRASH

Zealous, sustained giving breathed excitement and life into Billy and Emma's relationship and faith. They were thrilled they could help further God's work.

Then came 2008 and, along with it, a real estate crash in Southern California. Billy had invested in numerous properties, the value of which plunged virtually overnight. In just a few months, he and Emma went from having a couple million dollars in the bank to having a negative net worth.

Adding insult to injury, the money stopped rolling in. "In 2007," says Billy, "I had work contracts guaranteeing me a hundred thousand dollars a month. In one week in 2008, those contracts went down to *zero*. We lost all of them. Even though we had legal agreements, the companies said, 'Sue us,' and we had no perceptible income to pay a lawyer."

Though Billy was being cheated, it wasn't in him to cheat others. He refused to declare bankruptcy or renege on mortgage payments of properties now worth less than what he owed on them. "We believed that we signed those loans and therefore were obligated to pay them off. We gave our word and were determined to honor it."

"I looked at this like a faith lesson," Billy remembers, "so I worked myself crazy for the next six years and reduced every expense. We had a scorched-earth policy on expenses. I sold my $100,000 sports car and bought a used truck. We sold the properties as their value came back up, just to get out of the debt. We still had both kids going to private colleges, requiring an outlay of more than $100,000 a year. When we agreed to those tuitions, that $100,000 represented a month's income. Now it looked like a whole lot more than we'd earn in a year."

AN UNFULFILLED TESTIMONY

This next segment may make some of you angry or think I'm questioning faith, but I want to be honest. As we saw, Donna and Kirk's story had a happy ending. They got their spending under control, started tithing, and saw their income increase, and they now live debt-free lives. That hasn't been the case for Billy and Emma.

One of the things that fueled Billy's sense of sacrifice was his belief that there was no way they could outgive God. "We hadn't spent our way into debt, we had given our way into debt, in the sense that we gave instead of saved. Even so, we were claiming those promises that God would honor our giving. We expected to have a great testimony. We're still waiting on that testimony."

In the face of her disappointment, Emma became even more earnest about growing her faith through studying the Bible and reading books. One such book, *The Power of a Praying Wife* by Stormie Omartian,[45] led her to begin praying for Billy in a new way—as it related to their finances.

Being encouraged to pray about my husband's wisdom in handling finances and for his ability to increase revenue was a revelation for me. I had never really considered praying specifically for him in those areas. My previous prayers had been more generic, but now they became specific. I also prayed for wisdom so that when Billy asked me for my advice, I could give it to him. Doing that helped immensely in the sense that I felt we were facing this crisis together.

For her Bible study, Emma relished Psalm 23. She grew up with the King James Version—"The LORD is my shepherd; I shall not want"—but found new encouragement from the New Living Translation: "The LORD is my shepherd; I have all that I need."

"I was struck by the notion," says Emma, "that because God is my shepherd, I have everything I need."

Please notice that Emma believes she has everything she needs *because God is her shepherd*, not because Billy is her husband. Some financially stressed couples start to blame each other: "Why can't you earn more? Why aren't you better at handling our finances? Why can't you get a second job? Why did you spend that much?"

Emma's prayer life and Bible study kept her turning *to* God instead of *on* her husband. That's what has made their marriage a fortress, in spite of their ongoing need.

A SHORT REPRIEVE

Billy's hard work initially paid off and money started to flow back in again, so he and Emma went back to their reckless giving at the expense of their saving and investing. Just when they thought they could breathe again financially, the world shut down due to COVID-19. This hit was even more brutal to Billy's business than the 2008 real estate crash had been. His professional services were the first thing fearful companies shed. "I went from two hundred speaking dates a year to zero in a matter of weeks." At the urging of several of his clients, he had invested millions of dollars in developing online training that won industry awards, but in his business, if you're not traveling, you're not selling. He still hasn't seen a return on his huge investment. "COVID-19 scared everybody. Companies just stopped spending."

Things got so bad that Billy felt forced to sell the comfortable home they had raised their children in. "Selling our home relieved a lot of pressure for me, but it broke Emma's heart." Even so, Billy was thinking about Emma's future. "It's not just that I wanted to provide for her. I wanted to leave enough behind so that if something happened to me, Emma wouldn't be dependent on our kids or anyone else."

As I write this, Billy and Emma are still trying to ride out the effects of COVID-19 on their business. "There hasn't been your typical 'happily ever after' ending to our story. Some promises from Scripture haven't yet been realized."

Emma is leaning on Philippians 4:12–13 (NLT): "I know how to live on almost nothing or with everything. I have learned the secret of living in every situation, whether it is with a full stomach or empty, with plenty or little. For I can do everything through Christ, who gives me strength."

The difference in their marriage is that they really love each other, and the joy of their relationship is worth more to them than millions.

For Billy, this long-drawn-out experience (he was worth far more in his thirties than he is now as he approaches sixty) demanded what he calls a values clarification. He says, "I spent thirty years giving away a far greater percentage of my income than any parable would ask of me. If anybody asked us for help, our default answer was yes. Not once did I look at our balance sheet. I just expected God to take care of me and my wife as we got older. Now I feel guilty, knowing that Emma could have fifteen or twenty years of life without me, and I haven't guaranteed that her basic necessities will be met. I didn't expect to be wealthy my entire life, but I did expect to not be dependent on other people or have to lease a house from one of my children."

Today's church members can be quite selective about the promises we claim and proclaim. There are some words of Jesus we don't stick on our refrigerators:

> "In this world you will have trouble" (John 16:33).
> "Everyone will hate you because of me" (Luke 21:17).
> "I will show [Paul] how much he must suffer for my name" (Acts 9:16).
> "We must go through many hardships to enter the kingdom of God" (Acts 14:22).

We don't stress that though Jeremiah was righteous and faithful, he described his situation as "pain unending . . . my wound grievous and incurable" (15:18). This sacrificing servant of God was beaten and put in stocks (see 20:1–2), had his writings burned rather than published (see 36:20–32), and was arrested and put in a dungeon for "a long time" (37:16) where conditions were so terrible he thought to return there would mean his certain death (see 37:20). He was betrayed by his family, accosted by religious leaders, considered a traitor by his own government, and eventually handed over to his persecutors by a weak-willed king, Zedekiah (see 38:5). Ultimately, he was carted off to exile without ever seeing glorious success.

Author Frank Viola comforts and warns believers:

If you are called to the Lord's work, suffering has a specific meaning and purpose in your life.

Your personal manual for this is the book of 2 Corinthians, where Paul explains that the secret to life-giving ministry is the suffering that leads to brokenness and death to self . . .

If you are engaged in God's work, carnage awaits . . .

The Father's goal, then—in making a man or woman of God who can advance His kingdom—is brokenness and devastation to the self-life.

When God decides to break a man or a woman under His sovereign hand, that person may feel like choosing hell instead. It's supreme agony. Unmitigated torture.

And the blows can be unrelenting . . .

One of the greatest lessons that God wants to teach you on the obstacle course of the Christian life is to hold everything with a loose hand. To be willing to lose all you hold dear at a moment's notice, including everything you've built.

If you're going to have an impact in the kingdom of God, you will have periods when you are broken, shattered, beaten, and bloodied.[46]

LESSONS LEARNED

Let's pivot to some of the lessons Donna and Kirk learned as they faced their own financial challenges.

Kirk urges couples who finally realize how bad things are for them financially (like owing more money than you make in a year), "First, take a deep breath. The wheels aren't coming off. It's not the end of the world. You can get through this."

Donna stresses the need to tend to your marriage as you're reviewing your finances. She says, "Your marriage is more important than being angry and turning against each other or getting a divorce." Don't let a *financial* crisis become a *marital* crisis. Resolve that the challenge will bring the two of you closer and make you stronger rather than allowing it to tear you apart and make you weaker.

Forgive yourself and your spouse for the financial trouble you've gotten into. Jesus emphasized forgiveness (see Matthew 6:14–15; Mark 11:25; Luke 11:4), and Paul sums it up in Colossians 3:13: "Bear with each other and forgive one another if any of you has a grievance against someone. Forgive as the Lord forgave you."

Donna stresses, "If one of you is blaming the other, you've got to work through that to get it settled; you're in this *together*. You won't make it if you're not on the same page."

Kirk stresses, "You need to tithe. I don't care how big your debt is. I'm not a 'prosperity gospel' kind of guy—'Send me a seed faith offering, and God will send you a silk purse'—but the Bible teaches that God deserves the first cut. That may not lead to a raise—which is what happened for me—but tithing isn't about getting a raise; it's about giving to God what rightfully belongs to him in the first place."

Let me say that from a New Testament perspective, I can't teach that a 10 percent tithe is a legalistic rule that must be followed. The Old Testament priesthood is over, and Paul never legalistically renewed it for the churches he writes to. I believe it belongs with the Sabbath—a wise principle that is no longer a law (but still part of wise living). Jesus does refer to a tithe in Matthew 23:23 (see also Luke 11:42) and seems to commend it, but that was before his death and resurrection (and the launch of the new covenant) and is in the context of a scathing denunciation of the Pharisees being legalistic about tithing while ignoring weightier matters of the faith. Because of this, I don't fault pastors for urging tithing in a nonlegalistic fashion, just as I don't fault speakers who urge us to keep a Sabbath—as long as it's not a legalistic command. For most of us I think a tithe is a good starting point to check our own hearts and to make sure we don't see our money as our own.

Donna urges couples to get help and is especially partial to Financial Peace University. Donna says she has seen a marked improvement when couples apply Dave Ramsey's teachings. This program gave them the tools, says Donna, "to stop the bleeding, to be able to stop using credit cards, or at the very least, to pay off the balance every month. Get on a budget; figure out what you can and can't spend, and look for ways to bring in some extra income if you can. There are many more ways to do that these days."

They both stress that their greatest failure as a couple (apart from spending everything they earned and going into debt) was not being equally aware of their financial bottom line. Don't put financial solvency on either spouse. Because two people spend and save, two people need to know what's left and what's not, and how deep the hole is getting.

Among the things that Kirk and Donna felt they did right was turning to God in their scarcity. In hindsight, the best thing that came out of their financial hole was that it became a spiritual well, essentially forcing them to draw more deeply on the spiritual resources God offers to face a material challenge.

WE DID IT TOGETHER

What was once the source of Donna and Kirk's greatest pain in marriage—owing more money on credit cards than they earned in an entire year, with those credit card companies gouging them with 18 percent interest—became the seedbed of their greatest growth as a couple. Together they faced a monumental challenge, and together they've come out on the other side. Accomplishments like this bind husbands and wives in the same way teammates are drawn together by winning a championship.

"There is a great sense of accomplishment that we faced down a challenge that once seemed insurmountable, but by working together, we did it," says Donna. "And here's the thing: the fact that *we* did it means anybody can do it. We were determined from the very start that we would not let our financial debt bankrupt our marriage. We were determined to believe that we could prosper maritally even while struggling financially."

Facing this huge challenge together can grow your marriage. Let it! Talk, plan, forgive, and find a way to laugh.

Now that they're on the other side, Donna and Kirk enjoy their current affluence all the more. "The things we do have—that are all paid for!—mean that much more to us. Sometimes we stand in awe of how God has blessed us. And we love being able to travel. Memories are so much more wonderful than things. Our kids don't remember the stuff, but they do remember the memories we made on vacation."

LESSONS LEARNED
IN DEPRIVATION

For Emma and Billy, the lessons are a little different. They don't have a triumphal moment to share. But here's how the lack of resolution is still building their marriage:

> Emma and I had big, big dreams when we got married. Many of those financial dreams have not been realized, but we've been blessed a thousandfold in nonmaterial ways, with how God has used us to bless others and especially with our children and grandchildren. Blessings can be financial or represent things that are far more important than money. When it comes to nonmaterial blessings, we're not just billionaires; we're trillionaires. God fulfills his promises how he wants and when he wants, and I say that with reverence. Even though we're renting our home at a point in our lives when we thought we'd have at least one home paid off entirely, we wouldn't trade places with anybody. If we can eventually climb to the place of just having an average financial situation for people in their early sixties, we would feel like the most blessed people on the planet.
>
> Second, I've learned that the kind of teaching you hear on television doesn't always work out as promised. We gave not just generously but sacrificially, and because of that teaching, we expected that our generosity would be met with a new book contract, a business connection, some kind of financial favor to cover our stepping out in faith. Instead, God let us sacrifice to help others. Looking back, I think I would have saved and invested a little more.

I don't disagree with Billy's conclusion about wise saving and investing, but I would also encourage him with Jesus' assurances about heavenly rewards. Billy and Emma haven't been paid back for their generosity *yet*, but Jesus assures them that they will be: "Store up for yourselves treasures in heaven, where moths and vermin do not destroy, and where thieves do not break in and steal" (Mathew 6:20).

Billy understands this, as evidenced by what he told me:

God does not live within our time frame. A thousand years is like a day to him. It's a laughable joke to hold God to a timetable. Am I going to be joyful, comfortable with God providing for Emma, even if I'm not the vehicle he uses? I'm learning to live joyfully in the unfulfilled promises of God, but it's still something I struggle with every day. In one moment, I'm okay with it, and in the next moment, I take it back and am grinding again. Sometimes I feel sorry for myself. We gave all that money away, and this is what our kids and friends see us with now?

Perhaps the hardest challenge for Billy and Emma isn't how they have to endure financial deprivation but what it has cost them relationally. Sadly, they lost a number of friends when they couldn't pick up the dinner check anymore, pay for the golf fees, or take them on vacations. Other friends just grew tired of hearing about their struggles—not that they gripe or complain. They rarely bring it up themselves, but when asked, they are honest, and when their friends hear that nothing has changed, Billy says that "it's sort of like having a chronic illness. They only want to hear about healing."

For Billy, the experience has been humbling. "It's humiliating to feel like I can't take care of my own business. I've helped wealthy couples save billions of dollars by keeping them out of divorce court. I've helped Fortune 500 companies increase their revenues by millions of dollars, but I can't afford to own my own home."

Donna and Kirk learned how to get out of the hole they had dug for themselves, but Billy and Emma are learning the most difficult lesson of perseverance, which James taught is an essential aspect of Christian maturity: "Let perseverance finish its work so that you may be mature and complete, not lacking anything" (James 1:4).

The only way to learn perseverance is to keep going *when it keeps hurting*. You can't learn perseverance when life is easy. If perseverance is essential for us to be mature and complete, and if God wants us to be mature, then he can't allow life to always be easy. That would be like a head coach who brings doughnuts to every practice and tells their players to lounge around in the sun instead of work out.

Billy's struggles are a sobering reminder that we don't (as one classical writer put it) get to choose our own crosses. God chose to teach Donna and Kirk the key to self-control and generous giving. Billy and Emma had learned both of those skills, so God is using the lack of finances to teach them perseverance in a way few will know.

I was most moved by something Emma told me near the end of our interview. Rather than questioning Billy—as some of their friends and even their children occasionally do—she has found that her respect for him has grown, and she actively seeks to protect his reputation. When a friend of Emma's asked them about "purchasing" their most recent house—the one they actually rented from their son—Emma found a way to not lie but also not disclose the rental agreement so that the person wouldn't think less of Billy.

Some Christians still live with the Old Testament mindset, shared by the early disciples, that financial prosperity is a sign of God's favor with who you are and what you're doing, just as poverty is a sign of God's curse. That faulty worldview explains why the disciples were "greatly astonished" when Jesus told them it is "hard for someone who is rich to enter the kingdom of heaven" (Matthew 19:23, 25). Jesus' simple phrase upset everything they had been taught and believed—a worldview that, again, many modern Christians still hold to: Tithe, and you'll never be in want. Be faithful and holy, and you're guaranteed an above-average, affluent life. As shared earlier, this is not an absolute biblical promise. Emma not only respects Billy but wants others to respect him too, so she's very careful about what she shares. She wants this season of perseverance to build her husband up rather than discourage him even more than it already has.

In addition to respecting and encouraging her husband, Emma faced the sale of her kids' childhood home without bitterness. "I knew our debts were an overwhelming burden on Billy, and that the proceeds from selling the house would be like lifting a stinking albatross that was hanging around his neck twenty-four hours a day. I loved that home, but I love Billy more. How could I take joy in something that was causing so much pain to my husband and that might threaten my marriage?"

Emma urges other wives to follow her example. "In our world, how one does financially is part of a man's image. Though

I disagree with that, I don't want others who do believe that to negatively judge Billy or see him in a bad light. Be careful about who you share your struggles with. Some things should be kept within your marriage or within a small circle of trusted friends who can pray for you over these matters."

Just as Emma seeks to protect Billy, he is all about urging husbands to protect their wives' security. This doesn't have to be gender based, of course, but in their case (since Emma no longer earns an income), Billy wishes he would have handled their finances better—in the sense of saving and investing and perhaps not giving away so much—for Emma's sake, not his own. He grieves the loss of the home Emma loved. He wishes she understood that if he dropped dead, she'd never have to get a job or ask for a handout. He'd tell younger husbands to keep their wives' welfare and sense of security in mind as they balance giving and saving.

Billy and Emma's financial story on earth doesn't have a happy ending yet, and may never have, but that's real life. We all see good people die young every day, while evil people seem to prosper and live beyond their years.

Money, or the lack thereof, will either curse or bless your relationship. You get to choose. How you look at money and how you handle your money *together* will determine its impact on your marriage, far more than whether you have too much or seemingly not enough.

> You have been a refuge for the poor,
>> a refuge for the needy in their distress,
> a shelter from the storm
>> and a shade from the heat. (Isaiah 25:4)

Building Your Fortress Takeaways

1. Both affluence and financial deprivation can strengthen marriages if they are faced together. Finances impact a marriage, but they needn't define it—through either prosperity or times of want.

2. For the sake of ongoing marital intimacy, it's essential that both spouses know the basics about their financial bottom line—what they have saved, what they owe, what they are giving away.

3. Being angry isn't a sin, but it can lead us into sin. You're not disobeying Scripture by going to bed when you're still angry but too tired to keep talking it out. Sometimes the wisest choice is to deal with the conflict when you're better rested.

4. If you're trying to climb out of a debt hole, planning together and making sacrifices can grow your marriage even as you shrink your debt.

5. Being financially strapped for the first decade of their marriage didn't negatively affect Billy and Emma's relationship because their expectations were under control. They didn't expect life to be easy, and so they weren't resentful when it wasn't.

6. When you're going through difficult seasons, your attitude more than the circumstances will make life sweet or bitter.

7. Character matters more to God (and should matter more to us) than wealth, so we can expect difficult times in life. The times of challenge are acts of love on God's part, not of indifference or malice.

8. Giving your money away doesn't always guarantee financial security. It's not unwise to consider saving for the future.

9. Increase your emotional and spiritual connection with your spouse by praying specific prayers for their ability to earn and prosper.

10. Find refuge and comfort in the truth of Psalm 23—that you have everything you need because God is your shepherd, not because of what your spouse is able to provide.

11. Many couples have felt overwhelmed by their debt burden, but by working together, cutting expenses, growing their income, and giving to God, they have found their way to the other side.

12. Don't let a financial crisis become a marital crisis. The marriage matters more than your bank account. Face the challenge together in a forgiving, encouraging way.

13. The accomplishment of overcoming a major financial challenge together can build great marital intimacy.

14. The "give to get" line of teaching doesn't always pan out. Sometimes God allows us to sacrifice and reserves the rewards for eternity.

15. There's no spiritual maturity without perseverance. There's no growth in perseverance without pain.

CHAPTER 8

· · · · · · · · · · · · · ·

REBUILDING YOUR FORTRESS

Overcoming Past Hurts with
Truth and Transparency

Note: *this chapter deals with a husband's journey out of sexual addiction. If either you or your spouse is currently facing this challenge, some of the details of this story may be triggering for you, and you may want to skip this chapter.*

Note that this account was written after the husband had gone through years of counseling and active recovery. The teachings here should not be thought of as advice for couples who are currently struggling with this issue. If your spouse is facing an active addiction, I recommend you seek individual counseling for yourself from a professional who understands sex addiction and betrayal trauma so that you can be properly cared for. Your spouse's addiction is not a marital issue in the sense that you each bear responsibility.

This chapter is still relevant for couples who haven't faced an addiction in that it provides a helpful look at how we need to address deep hurts from the past to go forward in our marriage.

The Tour de France is a grueling three-week bike race that typically covers 3,500 kilometers (well over two thousand miles) in twenty-one days of racing. The last week almost always has definitive stages in the Alps or Pyrenees. Imagine cycling up a series of mountain ranges *after* your body has already been beaten down from two weeks of racing over other mountains and long stretches of road.

You can't fully prepare for this kind of race. You can ride your bike over Alpe d'Huez during the off-season, but how do you mimic doing that after your body has been systematically broken down by weeks of intense competition and you've been through a couple of crashes? The average rider has two and a half accidents during every major tour; thus many riders are continuing to race with painful road rashes and even broken bones at times.

Marriage can be like the third week in the Tour de France in that many of us limp into it after a lifetime of hurt. We're broken down before we get to the starting line. Few people (maybe none) escape childhood without some scars—sexual abuse, parental neglect, bullying, romantic betrayal, and the list goes on. We've often been hurt deeply and are sometimes weakened before we enter marriage, just when we'll face new challenges—spiritually, relationally, and emotionally.

Of course, we also bring many relational gifts into marriage. Some of you received a legacy of faith, secure love, and affirming encouragement from your family of origin. These should be celebrated every bit as much as our early scars should be named, evaluated, and brought into the healing presence and grace of Jesus, the healer of our souls. If we want to make our marriage a fortress, we have to deal with our past hurts or else risk letting them bleed into our current relationship.

TWO HURTING PEOPLE

Roxanne suffered one of the greatest wounds of her life when her dad left their family when she was a young girl. His leaving left her "damaged and heartbroken," so she told her husband, Keith, "Please don't *ever* do that to me." Because of her family of origin story, Roxanne always believed that divorce wasn't an option for her. She didn't want her children to know the searing pain of a broken family. But even more than Roxanne was anti-divorce, she was anti-affairs, as it had been an affair that ripped her dad from her mom. She warned Keith, "I could never stay with someone who cheated on me."

Keith also stumbled into marriage with a hurting soul. He grew up as a middle child and was often on his own. He almost never spent time alone with either of his parents. Genuine intimacy was hard for him to come by. His intimacy disorder became immeasurably worse when at age eleven, he was sexually assaulted by another boy.

"I was really small for my age and emotionally immature. I didn't know how to handle what had happened to me, so I blocked it out of my mind completely and tried to forget it had even happened."

A seasoned licensed counselor with considerable experience in this area told me that when he hears of a boy being molested, he just waits for "all the dominoes to fall" as he hears the rest of his story. He can practically paint the picture of addiction that will follow, even before his client reveals their personal story.

Keith's childhood trauma does not excuse his adult behavior. Childhood trauma never does. But it helps us understand Keith's behavior. People are complicated, and while childhood wounds don't necessarily lead to adult addictions, they certainly can prime the pump.

Keith never told anyone what had happened. As is commonly the case when young children are molested, he thought it was partly his fault—now, as an adult, he knows that's not even partly true. Building on the molestation was Keith's early exposure to pornography that began when he was just eight years old. More than Keith was motivated by lust, he was motivated by relationship. "Even back then, I think I was seeking out affirming relationships," he says. "I just wanted people to tell me I was special or okay because I never got that affirmation at home. Being able to please a woman affirmed me in a way I never knew before."

The relationship component carried through Keith's adult life. He looked at porn up until he got married and stopped for a while, but when the internet became the phenomenon it is today, his old habit became a present terror. It wasn't just visual porn, however. Since he was motivated by intimacy more than lust, he began to talk to women online, which is what led him to do what Roxanne had begged him never to do, what she said she could never forgive—have multiple affairs.

Keith explains, "It was less about lust and more about affirmation. How could I feel better about myself?" For him, more than he craved the visual nature of porn, he wanted "somebody to tell me how smart or nice I was."

When he finally went to a recovery group in Houston, Keith didn't describe himself as a sex addict; he described himself as a relationship addict. Keith's story underscores that a healthy sex life doesn't stave off or fix addictive sexual behavior. Dr. Jake Porter, a licensed professional counselor in Houston, Texas, specializes in sexual addiction.[47] He explained:

One way to think of sex addiction is as a disordered attachment. God's design for sex is that it is a means of connecting to a person, the person to whom we give ourselves in the covenant of marriage. In God's beautiful design, sex strengthens and reinforces our attachment to our covenant partners. But when someone is addicted to sex, their attachment system (usually through trauma) has reversed the ends and the means such that a *person* becomes the means and *sex* becomes the end. They are attached to the experience of sex, and they use a person (or people—in the flesh or digitally) to get it. This is like in Romans 1 where the order of creation is reversed, when the Creator is exchanged for the created thing.[48]

In my Cherish seminars, I talk about the difference between using sex to cherish our spouse and using our spouse to cherish sex. Dr. Porter provides the professional understanding behind that dynamic in the context of his counseling.

Keith and Roxanne's sex life satisfied both of them for the most part, but deception was part of the allure for Keith. It created an endorphin-laced emotional component that a healthy marriage couldn't match. Again, addiction often seeks a *dysfunctional* kind of sex that a spouse in a healthy relationship can't provide. Keith needed to get healed first. Nothing his wife might do or provide could make the hurt—or his behavior—simply go away.

Personal dysfunction isn't always related to sex, of course. Let's make this a little more general so that those who don't face this particular issue can still find something to take away. Instead of just focusing on the behavior of a dysfunction, explore what's behind it. Ask yourself:

Why am I so insecure?

Why am I so jealous?

Why am I so needy for affirmation?

Why do I get so angry if I don't feel respected?

Why do I need to find solace in eating or spending money when my spouse doesn't notice me?

A gifted licensed counselor can help you prayerfully explore the answers to these questions. These unresolved issues aren't just assaulting you; they're assaulting your marriage. Asking these deeper questions of yourself and persevering until you have an answer are almost always far more productive exercises than asking your spouse, "Why do you make me feel insecure? Why do you act in ways that make me feel jealous? Why can't you appreciate me? Why do you make me so angry?"

Dysfunction rooted in our unaddressed past can't be blamed on what our spouse is doing or not doing today. On the contrary, our tendency to stray, to become angry, or to feel insecure can be rooted in life experiences that occurred long before we even met, much less married, our spouse. If we do this personal spiritual work outside of our marriage—examining our motives, meeting with a licensed counselor if necessary, receiving forgiveness and healing—we gain a renewed understanding of who we are, why we do what we do, and why we feel what we feel. This is a gift to our sense of well-being, but it's also a gift to our spouse, who will be blessed by our newfound peace and presence. If we fail to deal with unaddressed areas in our life, we can erode our marriage rather than making it a fortress. Roxanne could love Keith, but she couldn't fix him.

Understanding our past and how it has imprinted us and still affects us today is a key component of being liberated from that past. The truth will set us free—not exactly what Jesus meant in context in John 8:32, but true nonetheless.

TRUTH IS A TREASURE

Character flaws are like floodwaters running over a bank. You can't contain where the waters (or behaviors) go. If you're an angry person, you'll be angry as a parent, friend, sibling, spouse, and coworker. If you're deceptive about one thing, you'll likely be deceptive about other issues too. Roxanne remembers, "We were poor, and Keith would tell me he had paid a bill, but then I'd find out he hadn't. That's when I became aware my husband could lie. And if he could lie about paying a bill, he could lie about having sex with someone else."

I can't stress enough how truth serves as a foundation for marriage. *If we are not passionate about the truth, we cannot remain passionate about our spouse.* Love is fed by truth; lying is in reality a form of hatred that turns us against our spouse. Lying demolishes respect and welcomes fear into our hearts (the fear of being found out). It diminishes our spouse in our own minds (you can't respect someone you're lying to) and obliterates peace (how can you have peace while you're waiting to be found out?). You'll eventually resent your spouse and even want your spouse removed from your life to avoid the consequences of having lied to them.

If you're hiding your food wrappers, burying expenses, throwing bottles away in a place where your spouse can't find them, or making up lies about where you really were, you are already, in a spiritual sense, divorcing your spouse. *If you want your marriage to be a fortress against the storms of life, find refuge in the truth.* The first thing Paul urged us to fix our minds on is *the truth* (Philippians 4:8). As soon as we invite deception into our marriage, we're making our fortress vulnerable from within.

If one characteristic marks a thought as Christian, it is that it is *true.* Jesus said, "I am the way and the *truth* and the life" (John 14:6, emphasis added). If one characteristic marks a thought as demonic, it is that it is a lie: "You belong to your father, the devil, and you want to carry out your father's desires. He was a murderer from the beginning, not holding to the truth, for there is no truth in him. When he lies, he speaks his native language, for he is a liar and the father of lies" (John 8:44). Notice how lying and murder go hand in hand. Lying is to a relationship what murder is to the body.

"My deception was a long downward spiral," Keith confesses. "I'd explain away conversations, or even lie about how I was supposedly finishing college when I wasn't."

The deception became easier when Keith switched jobs and started traveling internationally. The distance and time zone changes gave him a lot of free time without any observation. It was on one of those trips that he developed a relationship with a coworker. Again, once you breach the channel, character flaws can start to run wild. When he got home, he also cheated with a neighbor, who happened to be one of Roxanne's childhood friends. The escalating behavior into something worse and worse is typical of an addict.

Roxanne knew the distance between Keith and her was becoming overwhelming when, on their twenty-fifth anniversary, Keith didn't even give her a gift. It's impossible to cherish your spouse if you're harboring an addiction, because addiction sucks up all your energy and focus into itself. Today, Keith can't even imagine being the kind of guy who wouldn't give a gift on such a milestone anniversary.

His downward spiral continued until during one heated argument on the phone, Keith got mad and hung up.

Roxanne sent him an angry text back, after which Keith texted, "I'm done."

"What?"

"I'm done."

In Keith's mind, their marriage was over. Deception had done its work and completely murdered Keith's affection for his wife.

Roxanne remembers, "I cried so hard. And then I asked myself, *Who is it? There has to be somebody else.*"

She remembered an incident six months before when she was walking to the game room upstairs and overheard him talking on his cell phone. "He was whispering and talking nicely, in a tone I used to hear but now never did. I started tiptoeing to get closer, but then he hung up. When I asked him who he was talking to, he gave the name of a friend, whom I immediately texted and asked, 'Was Keith just on the phone with you?'"

The one-word answer from the friend almost exploded everything: "No."

"All right, then," Roxanne asked Keith on the spot, "who *were* you talking to?"

Keith was caught. If he had confessed and started living by the truth, they could have started putting their marriage back together months before they did. But Keith stuck with his deception and lied. "It was a coworker, but we were just talking about work."

Roxanne was so upset that she left the house and drove around the neighborhood while sobbing. Yet she still couldn't believe her husband would do to her what her dad had done to her mom.

He just wouldn't. She knew he had lied to her, but she refused to believe he would actually have an affair.

Do you see how Keith's childhood wounds set him up to one day assault his own marriage? Do you see how Roxanne's childhood wounds were worsened by the discovery of Keith's betrayal? If you want to make your marriage stronger, you may need to go back to what happened to you long before you got married. You need to be set free from your past—or at least understand how it is affecting you, compelling you, and sometimes haunting you—before you can carve out a new future.

I want to stress that this kind of counseling isn't always about fixing your marriage or spouse. There's nothing Roxanne could have done to get Keith not to cheat. He was going to be unfaithful regardless.

THE BURNING FUSE

Throughout the whole time that Keith was cheating on Roxanne, he didn't want to lose her. That might be difficult for some to understand, but most counselors get this. Keith was messed up emotionally and spiritually, battling a seemingly overpowering sense of shame, loneliness, and a lack of self-control by choosing some wicked and foolish diversions, but deep in his heart, even though he said, "I'm done," he didn't really want to lose Roxanne. He just felt it was inevitable that he *would* lose her because of what he was doing and thought he might as well just get it out of the way, forcing her hand with outrageous behavior.

One of Keith's affairs was with a woman whom Roxanne had known in high school. She and Roxanne reunited as their kids swam together during the day. In the evenings, this friend and Keith worked on local theater projects together, and that's when the affair erupted.

Roxanne remembers, "She started treating me poorly and I started getting really uncomfortable around her, but I never imagined it was because she was sleeping with my husband."

Lying kills more than marriages; it kills all relationships. You can't maintain intimacy with someone you're lying to. Lying unleashes spiritual forces that go hand in hand with hatred, resentment, and disrespect because lying usually *is* a form of hatred, resentment, and disrespect.

Dr. Porter explains:

When I withhold the truth from my wife, I actually take from her the ability to make a choice in response to her real reality. I allow her to believe in a false reality and make choices according to that. This is incredibly disempowering to her, and it puts me in a one-up position. I know all the data; she doesn't. What makes betrayal really sting is the withholding of information that if it had been known might have prompted someone to choose otherwise. It steals a person's sense of agency. One thing this means is that I wonder what would happen if my partner did get all the facts. Would she still choose me and our relationship? This uncertainty fuels the fear and shame that drive addictive acting out in the first place.

After Roxanne got the "I'm done" text, she reached out a couple days later by sending her own text. She now knew that Keith was having some kind of affair (though she didn't know it was with her friend), so she texted him:

> You know God will never bless what you're doing. I saw my dad
> go through three marriages, and then he had a heart attack.
> You'll never be happy if you keep going in this direction. But if
> you'll get out of this and promise to never do it again, you can
> come home.

Keith returned home but still "felt like the *Mission: Impossible* fuse was burning. I knew my wife would find out about *everything* I had done; it was just a matter of time. I think I was trying to distance myself to prepare myself for her leaving. After all, she had warned me that if I did what I had already done—though she didn't know it yet—she would leave me."

Even when they started going to counseling, Keith continued to lie. Once again, the story of this chapter is that *truth is the refuge your marriage needs*. Today, at every point in their story, Keith wishes he would have come clean months, even years, before he did. At the time, lying seemed like a good strategy. Now he recognizes that lying made things immeasurably worse and multiplied the hurt he caused his wife—the love of his life—immensely.

If you want to make your marriage a fortress, stop lying right now.[49] Keep in mind, honesty is a journey. Recklessly sharing something you know might hurt your spouse can itself be abusive. If you have something to share that could unleash trauma, talk it over with a counselor beforehand to strategize about the proper way and time to speak the truth.

Keith couldn't get healthy as long as he was lying. Which is why it's not surprising that Keith reached out once again to the coworker with whom he had an affair. Dr. Porter told me, "One thing that makes addiction addiction is that someone wants to stop the behavior, tries to stop it, and can't. This is a miserable process, which as both a recovering addict and addiction professional, I can personally attest to. An important marker of addiction is progression or escalation of behaviors. Sex addicts continually break their own boundaries with themselves. This is a major source of the shame that actually ends up fueling their addiction."

While pastors like me often talk about people "falling" into temptation, Keith experienced *compulsion* that felt like a loss of control. That's a different dynamic altogether.

The woman Keith reached out to sent Roxanne a text, telling her that Keith was still trying to contact her. And she also filled Roxanne in on the details. While Keith had told the counselor the two of them had been actively seeing each other for just a couple months, the coworker told Roxanne it had been a full year.

If you've been cheating, it's likely that your spouse will hear from the one you're cheating with. Sometimes they'll do it out of spite because they are angry you cut them off. Maybe they'll become convicted and want to come clean to clear their own conscience. Or they might do it out of bitterness because you're not leaving your spouse, hoping to force your hand. I've seen it happen so often. Truth be told, I'm astonished that offending spouses are surprised when their illicit partner outs them. More often than not, it's inevitable.

ANATOMY OF A CHEATING HEART

Before we look at how this couple survived Keith's affairs, let's chart how things went wrong. Our review will highlight takeaways for every marriage, even those that aren't dealing with sexual addiction or a cheating spouse.

We've already talked about Keith's sense of alienation from his immediate family, the childhood molestation, and his social anxiety that left him desperate for intimacy. He didn't believe he deserved to be married to a strong Christian. Childhood trauma and the decision to believe a lie made it easy for Keith to dive headfirst into sinful behavior. It's wise for all of us to consider the effects of past trauma and the lies we are tempted to believe.

"I knew Roxanne was different and special, unlike anyone else I knew. I also knew that I didn't deserve her and figured that if she knew who I really was, she wouldn't stay married to me. That sense of unworthiness haunted me and put me on a relational spiral, not unlike an alcoholic who starts out with one drink, then two, and on it goes. No matter how far down the scale you've gone, I had to escalate it to address the growing pain."

Rochelle, another wife who has been cheated on, told me, "I heard as many times as I went to therapy that 'this is not about you.' That's something Doug reminds me of many times. Our instinct as wives is to assume we weren't delivering enough to keep our husbands content. It's a flat-out lie when Satan says, 'If you had only been [fill in the blank], this would not have happened.'

"After going through so much trauma, the last thing a wife needs is blame. Doug's addiction was in place well before I came into the picture. I couldn't have done anything to prevent it, and there wasn't anything I could have done to keep him from acting out, because *it wasn't about me.*"

Doug, her husband, agrees. "The biggest misconception about a husband's affair is that a guy is trying to find something *better.* I was trying to find something in *myself* that I couldn't deal with; I never wanted to replace my marriage or my family. When it all exploded, my questions were, 'What's real? Who am I? What do

I really want in my life?' I was able to see that I wanted a life with Rochelle and our children more than anything else."

The same thing seemed to be true with Keith. Yet his deceptions became increasingly worse. "I was unfaithful from the beginning of our marriage in escalating ways."

Several sordid one-night encounters set him up to have a full-fledged, one-year affair with a coworker. Which set him up to have an affair with his wife's close friend. It just kept getting worse.

This is the pattern of deception. Once you start down that slope and "get away" with something, the action that follows tends to be worse the next time. And if you get away with that, you go further down the hole until you can't see much light anymore. Keith freely admits, "I was always going just a little further after swearing not to do what I had already done."

Dr. Porter explains that one of the markers of true addiction is the progression of acting-out behaviors. This is one of the ways you can distinguish true addictive acting out from typical affairs. It's important to note that with Keith, we're talking about an addict, not just a guy who looked at porn or had some affairs. *Any* porn use or *any* affair launches horrendous betrayal trauma on a spouse, so I'm not trying to minimize that at all. But understanding the nature of addiction is essential for the addict to get proper treatment.

SHOULD I STAY OR SHOULD I GO?

For pastors and friends reading this, let's not forget that the biggest victim in these circumstances is the spouse who is betrayed. Their healing and safety need to be our first concern, even over whether the marriage continues. Asking a woman to minimize what happened by living in close proximity to a husband whose behavior has traumatized her is cruel. A rather high percentage of women who discover such behavior experience posttraumatic stress disorder (PTSD), which is often associated with betrayal trauma.

This is an individual issue more than a marital one. We have to treat two traumatized individuals—both the addicted partner and the betrayed partner—before even asking the question of whether the marriage can continue. Teachers like me have done much harm in the past by focusing too much on the husband (assuming he is the one who has strayed; as we've seen in another story in this book, it can go either way) and his perceived need to be supported so he doesn't reoffend, while essentially ignoring the wife's need to heal and deal with her own trauma, not to mention make a reasoned decision about whether she can continue in the marriage.

Roxanne made a choice after a full therapeutic disclosure had occurred and her husband was in counseling and had agreed to an accountability process. Dr. Porter adds, "I want to strongly advocate for making clear that couples should *not* attempt a disclosure on their own, as this will likely result in more deception, minimization, and trauma. Men coming out of the fog of true addiction, even if their intentions are the best, will not be fully honest in a disclosure that is facilitated on their own. They likely aren't yet even being honest with themselves. Having a professional guide this process is crucial."

After this arduous and wrenching process, Roxanne remembers, "I had to decide whether to walk away because I figured it's over anyway or, once I knew what I was really facing, whether God would point to a path that could lead to repairing my marriage."

Both Roxanne and Keith found themselves crying out with the psalmist, "My eyes are fixed on you, Sovereign LORD; in you I take refuge—do not give me [or my marriage] over to death" (Psalm 141:8).

When your marriage is crumbling from your or your spouse's actions, make God your first refuge. Your God is for you, even if your spouse is not. Your spouse may not be capable of meeting your needs or even acknowledging your needs. Indeed, your spouse may be the source of your greatest hurt and frustration. Let the new distance in your marriage motivate you to increase your dependence on and intimacy with God. He gets you, even when your spouse doesn't. He loves you, even when your spouse hates you. He isn't done with you, even though your spouse may be. He sees your hurt, even though your spouse may be callous to the way they have traumatized you. Sharing all this with your God in prayer is far more important right now than trying to talk these things out with your spouse.

Dr. Porter encourages the couples he works with to acknowledge that the "old marriage actually is dead, but we serve a God who raises the dead. And just as Jesus was raised with the same body, but glorified, and just as we will be raised in the same bodies, but glorified, so marriage can be dead and then raised again, glorified."

Keith admits, "God is the most important thing. If you don't do business with God in your life right now, your marriage has zero chance of surviving. Zero. That's where I had to get to. After I had to disclose everything I had done to Roxanne, I thought our marriage had maybe a 1 percent chance of surviving. But I also knew that without disclosure, there would be a *zero* percent chance of our marriage surviving."

Keith had tried lying before and finally realized it only made things worse.

I asked Roxanne why she wanted to take back a man who had done what she said she could never accept and who cheated with the one person she had told him never to cheat with.

"In spite of all he had done, I knew Keith had a good heart. Also, I wanted my family to stay intact. I didn't want my children to go through the pain I went through, so I told myself, *I will suffer and do whatever it takes so my boys are not hurt*." To the glory of God, she now enjoys a rich intimacy with her husband, birthed by his full repentance, ongoing honesty, and accountability. She feels blessed as a wife.

Sharing this story of success is not intended to make wives whose husbands refused to repent and come clean feel guilty if their marriages didn't survive.[50] Some women (and men) believe they set a better example for their children by standing up against marital unfaithfulness, especially when the spouse says they're sorry but fail to take any steps in a different direction. "Sorry" isn't within miles of "enough" when a spouse has been unfaithful. But with sincere, demonstrated repentance, an affair doesn't have to bring a marriage to an end. When an affair does end a marriage, however, the offended spouse should never be made to feel guilty. Since Jesus himself presents adultery as grounds for divorce (see Matthew 5:32; 19:9), the church has no right to withhold what Jesus offers.

Another thing that helped Roxanne stay—and I think this is essential for every spouse who does decide to stay—is that she learned to look at Keith's actions through the lens of his hurt. Though the affairs hurt her, in the end she realized they weren't about her in the sense that Keith's actions weren't based on any supposition that she wasn't enough. She was more than enough;

she was his *ideal* wife! Keith's actions were motivated by his belief that *he* wasn't enough for her. He was deceived and in his deceit behaved abominably, but Roxanne believed an even better marriage could be had once they got to the other side, which is what they share today.

While Keith and Roxanne succeeded in saving their marriage, it's essential to point out that Keith was repentant, sought counseling (for years), was faithful in all his 12-step work, and agreed to be completely accountable (including taking ongoing polygraph tests). If you're married to a spouse whose unaddressed hurt leads them to keep hurting you, your response will be (and should be) very different.

ISOLATION

To this day, Keith believes his true spiritual downfall was isolation. Proverbs 18:1 (ESV) teaches, "Whoever isolates himself seeks his own desire; he breaks out against all sound judgment." Keith explains how this applied to him:

> Isolation is death. I wasn't honest with Roxanne or anyone. Not myself and not God. Back then, I didn't have any male friends and could never be honest with anyone. At root I strongly believed that if anyone found out who I really was, no one would want to have anything to do with me. So I lied to everyone.

How I wish our churches could be filled with authentic relationships in which people feel safe enough to share their fears and yet strong and wise enough to lead each other past them.

You strengthen your marriage by strengthening other relationships.

> Though one may be overpowered,
>> two can defend themselves.
> A cord of three strands is not quickly broken.
>> (Ecclesiastes 4:12)

> A friend loves at all times,
>> and a brother is born for a time of adversity.
>> (Proverbs 17:17)

Doug, the guy I mentioned earlier in this chapter, points out, "Addiction is so shame-based that it makes you want to hide from people, but being honest and vulnerable is the key to recovery and healing. I know every guy in my 12-step group really well—where they struggle, their character defects and strengths, their past, their family. But I may not know *anything* about their occupation, favorite sports team, or even their last name. At church it's just the opposite. I know all the surface stuff but none of the real stuff, none of the spiritual struggles."

Focusing only on our marriage relationship without increasing our relationship skills is very limiting, and something we men are particularly prone to do. We need to deepen the level of community in the local church if we want marriages to survive and thrive. The Bible invites us to deep participation in each other's lives: "Brothers and sisters, if someone is caught in a sin, you who live by the Spirit should restore that person gently . . . Carry each other's burdens, and in this way you will fulfill the law of Christ" (Galatians 6:1–2).

In response to my question about what Keith would tell his younger self, he says, "Don't isolate. Unless you are completely honest now and have controls in your life to stay that way, your pain will drive you to some terrible places. Many guys I've met in recovery have a molestation story, or at least really intense exposure to hardcore porn. None of us chose for that to happen, but then we made some very bad choices to deal with our pain that increased our angst rather than treated it."

He adds something else that is crucial. "If you've had an experience like mine, you need to get help. This is not something you can deal with on your own, nor can you expect your wife to understand it either. You need professional counseling to work through the horror and trauma and false guilt and emptiness. And if you've acted out, as I did, you need professional help to be wise about how and what you disclose to your wife. And then, of course, you need accountability that can lead to earning back your wife's trust."

If my car gets a flat tire, I can put on a spare. If my engine blows up, I need to call a mechanic. If you were a little too intimate with a high school crush, you probably don't need professional counseling to process what happened. If you felt like a family outcast, got into pornography at a young age, and then were molested, you're in way over your head. And you can't dump it on your spouse. Roxanne admits, "I wouldn't have been able to handle this if Keith hadn't gotten some help." Keith realized he needed to get help for *himself* first, not just for his marriage. Wise counselors can help you decide how much individual work must be done before couples counseling is recommended.

In addition to leaving isolation behind by getting help, Keith recommends developing guardrails. "Every spouse will be tempted. Temptation isn't sin; *acting on it* is. So put guardrails in place to safeguard you." The boundaries you need to help make your marriage a fortress will be unique to you. For Keith, they were things like this:

> Don't meet alone with someone of the opposite sex after work hours.
> Don't have personal conversations about your marriage with someone of the opposite sex.
> Check in with your spouse so they know where you are and what you are doing.

Author and speaker Joe Dallas gives invaluable advice by suggesting that once your walls have been breached—that is, you've already fallen—if you truly want to protect yourself, *you've got to make the next fall as close to impossible as you can get.* Having accountability software on every device in your house can go only so far if you're tech-savvy, so don't stop there. Ask or employ an even more tech-savvy person to set up the accountability system so you can't get around it.[51]

This may sound expensive, and embarrassing, but when my wife heard a pest control guy tell us we *already* had mice in the attic, the financial number that followed to keep them from getting into the house didn't even register with her. "Gary," she said, "write the check."

A cheating heart is much worse than gnawing mice. Value your marriage more than you value your money. If protecting your marriage isn't worth making a financial investment, it isn't that important to you.

Another way of "making a fall impossible" is to consider some conversations completely off-limits. Don't even start them. When a busy, ambitious man begins unloading his marital woes onto other women, he has already begun sliding down a treacherous mountain made of ice. Dr. Porter points out an interesting bit of developmental neuroscience: "Sharing secrets activates our biologically wired-in attachment systems. That's why people often have affairs with coworkers with whom they've gotten close. Once you start sharing stuff with someone that you aren't sharing with your spouse, you are messing with God's design and opening yourself to a misapplication of your attachment system, which is inextricably connected to your sexuality."

Also, remember that truth is wrapped in transparency. For many couples, sharing passwords and electronic devices is just part of being married. In my marriage, there's not one good reason I can think of that should make me hesitate to lend my iPhone or iPad to my wife, though a lot of bad reasons not to do so readily come to mind.*

EXPECT THE UNEXPECTED

Ancient fortresses that took hundreds of years to complete were often built to protect against one kind of attack, but by the time they were completed, there was an entirely new form of weaponry in use. Every day in our marriage, we are putting up bricks, shoring up foundations, adding another small layer to our fortress. We don't know which direction the enemy will attack from. We don't know how high our fortress must reach or even what weapons will be used against it. But we can make it a little stronger each day, confident that with God on our side, the fortress we build can withstand both a clever attack and a frontal assault.

---

* In an earlier chapter, I discussed that in situations where abuse and control are present, not sharing passwords can be wise and discerning. It's all about the motive.

We do that by fully engaging in our own soul work to understand our motivations, fears, desires, and weaknesses. And then we run with all our might to the God who can give us what our spouse really can't.

Proverbs 18:10 reminds us, "The name of the LORD is a fortified tower; the righteous run to it and are safe." This verse, along with Keith and Roxanne's encouragement to pray daily, provides a visual reminder to run to the fortified tower whose name is the Lord.

Our marital bricks are faith. Our mortar is the truth. Understanding our childhood hurts and responding with grace and empathy will give us the motivation to use marriage to overcome our past rather than repeat it. This has worked for so many people; it can work for you as well.

> Whoever fears the LORD has a secure fortress,
> and for their children it will be a refuge.
> (Proverbs 14:26)

Building Your Fortress Takeaways

1. Few people escape childhood without some significant psychological scars. If we want to make our marriage a fortress, we must deal with our past hurts or else risk allowing them to bleed into our current relationship.
2. An active sex life doesn't stave off or fix addictive sexual behavior. Present sexual enjoyment is usually powerless

against the dysfunction that follows skewed sexual programming from the past.

3. Our dysfunction rooted in an unaddressed past can't be blamed on what our spouse is or isn't doing today. On the contrary, our tendency to stray, to become angry, or to feel insecure can be rooted in life experiences that occurred long before we even met, much less married, our spouse.

4. We can't erase our past, but understanding our past and how it has imprinted us and still affects us today is a key component of liberation from that past.

5. Honesty is essential for building and maintaining marital intimacy. You cannot be truly intimate with someone you are lying to. Lying is to a relationship what murder is to the body.

6. If your spouse is engaged in addictive behavior, counseling is needed for each of you first, not for your marriage. You need to be cared for to become strong enough to learn how to respond appropriately and deal with your own trauma.

7. Your spouse's addiction isn't about you. It's not warranted or productive to wonder if you could have done something more or something less to stop them from acting out.

8. Character flaws of all kinds tend to escalate if they are not addressed and repented of. We promise not to do what we already did but then fall into something even worse.

9. The healing and safety of the spouse who has been victimized need to be prioritized even over the continuation of the marriage.

10. God can bring and has brought healing to broken marriages, but when an affair ends a marriage, the offended spouse shouldn't be made to feel guilty. Since Jesus himself presents adultery as grounds for divorce (see Matthew 5:32; 19:9), the church has no right to withhold what Jesus offers.

11. Try to see your spouse's actions through the lens of their past hurt. That doesn't excuse what they've done, but it can help you understand why they were tempted to do what they did, and it will allow you to make the choice to stay.

12. True spiritual downfall can begin with isolation. The church can support marriages by nurturing genuine communities of true fellowship and sharing.

13. Focusing only on your marriage relationship without increasing your relationship skills in general is limiting. Develop genuine relationships.

14. In cases of personal trauma, individual counseling is advised prior to marital counseling. You need a certain level of healing and victory on an individual basis before you can move on to address relational issues that may follow.

15. When you truly understand the seriousness of your past actions, you will work to make the next fall impossible.

CHAPTER 9

· · · · · · · · · · · · ·

FACING A CATASTROPHIC LOSS

The Power of Faith and Hope

Loss brings heartache. Catastrophic loss brings catastrophic heartache.

As a teen, I watched my mom grieve the death of her father. As a middle-aged man, I watched her grieve the death of her twin sister. My dad was a rock, in the best sense of the word, on both occasions, and their marriage grew because of it. Today, at ninety-three, he needs a walker to get around. He and my mom can't hold hands as they walk anymore, so my mom grips the handle of his walker as they move slowly around the mall. Just looking at them makes me want to cry.

Unfortunately, some marriages are buried alive by the avalanche of grief, and they never recover. Joe and Janell found a way to push forward in the face of the worst kind of loss. The testimony of their tenacity and grit can inspire and counsel couples facing any kind of loss.

THE FOUNDATION OF THEIR FORTRESS

If you talk with Joe on Zoom, his head is framed by a giant baseball jersey with the number 17. That was the number Joe's son, Garrett, wore as a celebrated high school catcher. Garrett was Joe and Janell's only child, a gifted boy with a promising future.

Everything changed on November 4, 2012, when Joe and Janell got the worst knock on their door you could ever imagine.

Garrett, their only child, was dead.

What prepared Joe and Janell for one of the most painful hits a marriage can take? How can a marriage survive not just the loss of a child but the loss of your only child?

Janell and Joe believe that making their marriage a fortress begins and ends with God. "We really hungered for the Word," Janell explains, "and both of us did *real* Bible studies, not just fluff studies."

Joe explains it this way: "We both took ownership of our spiritual walk. A friend of mine survived a terrifying plane engine failure and subsequent crash. When I asked him how he pulled himself through, he said, 'I had prepared and learned what to do when both engines failed. So when it actually happened, I knew what to do and I did it.'"

In a similar way, Joe and Janell's passion for the Word prepared their hearts to face the loss of their only son, even though, of course, they had no idea it would happen so soon and so cruelly.

In 2 Peter 1:5–8, Peter urges believers not to coast in their first faith:

> For this very reason, make every effort to add to your faith
> goodness; and to goodness, knowledge; and to knowledge,

self-control; and to self-control, perseverance; and to perseverance, godliness; and to godliness, mutual affection; and to mutual affection, love. For if you possess these qualities in increasing measure, they will keep you from being ineffective and unproductive in your knowledge of our Lord Jesus Christ.

Two elements to stress here: making "every effort" to grow instead of passively retiring into the security of your salvation, and possessing these qualities in "increasing measure." Joe and Janell wanted more knowledge, more self-control, more godliness, more maturity, and more love. They didn't know when or how they would need it, but having been faithful to Peter's teaching by seeking after it, they had the spiritual maturity they needed when they needed it. This kept them from being "ineffective and unproductive" in their knowledge of Jesus just when they needed him the most.

If you want your marriage to be a fortress against any assault, this indeed is the place to start.

> "The LORD is my rock, my fortress and my deliverer;
>   my God is my rock, in whom I take refuge,
>   my shield and the horn of my salvation.
> He is my stronghold, my refuge and my savior."
>   (2 Samuel 22:2–3)

To get and stay close to your spouse, focus first on getting and staying close to your God.

In times of happiness and health, it is so easy to amble along, spiritually speaking, not sinking our roots in worship, prayer, and Bible study because it doesn't feel like we need them. Our light faith can handle light trials. The danger is that we don't know if we're going to face an uncommon trial. Perhaps that's why the apostle Paul warns us, "Therefore let anyone who thinks that he stands take heed lest he fall" (1 Corinthians 10:12 ESV).

I started this book with a warning that times of testing will come for everyone. They *will* come for you. Are you growing your faith, your wisdom, and your maturity so you'll have the spiritual resources you need when they do? Growing deeper in Scripture, building faith relationships, and strengthening your faith spiritually is like buying a generator before hurricane season hits, stocking up on groceries, and making sure you have a plentiful supply of water. It's just a wise, practical thing to do.

A TIGHT UNIT

Just as much as they needed a strong *faith* to survive this hit, Joe and Janell needed a strong *union*. Janell's mom served as the role model of a woman who put her husband first, second only to her love for Jesus, but that's not what Joe had seen modeled. In fact, Joe's family presented a bit of a red flag to Janell when they first started dating. Joe is the youngest of his siblings, and all of them have now gone through at least one divorce (some have experienced several). Janell saw how Joe's siblings deferred to his mother over their spouses. "That became a breaking point for Joe and me," says Janell. "His mother was wonderful and she loved the Lord, but the concept of leaving and cleaving wasn't a part of Joe's family framework. I didn't think a marriage could survive without that."

In order to become his wife, Janell expected to come first in Joe's loyalty, even over his mother. Joe's mom may have sensed this, and she urged Joe not to marry Janell. Eventually, after eighteen months of dating, Joe and Janell broke up in large part due to the pressure from Joe's mom.

While Janell was deeply saddened over the breakup, she realized it was the right decision. Joe was a good man of faith, but Janell was not going to be the number two woman in any man's life.

Janell's strong, confident reaction to the breakup increased Joe's affection for his former girlfriend. "Janell is a very strong, intelligent, driven, and capable woman. My mom envisioned me marrying a nice, quiet, obedient, and subservient housewife. I decided my mother and I had different goals for my marriage, but my mom wasn't going to be married to Janell; I was!"

Over the next six months, Joe did a lot of soul-searching, until he went to his parents and said, "I made a big mistake when I broke up with Janell. I don't care what it costs me, but I'm going to get back with her if she'll have me."

His mom wasn't impressed. "I forbid you to get back with her," she said.

Joe laughed—spontaneously, not in a rebellious or cruel way. He had an excellent relationship with both parents. "Mom, I'm thirty-one years old. You know my background, my faith, my beliefs, and my walk with the Lord. I'm not entering into this marriage lightly. You know I decided not to date in law school because I wanted to focus on getting ready for my career. This isn't a spur-of-the-moment decision. I've given it due consideration, and I think your evaluation of Janell is just plain wrong. I'm an adult, and I'm going to make my own decisions."

Joe reached out to Janell, and when she agreed to meet, he laid it out: "I told my parents I'm ready to walk away and marry you. Even if they don't support it, I still choose you."

That was in July. They got engaged in August after Janell was convinced that Joe really would "leave" in order to "cleave." As a sign to Janell that the foundation of their marriage was to be their faith in Jesus, Joe asked Janell to marry him in the quiet, intimate chapel of their church. No video. No big show. Just a sincere, heart-felt entreaty: Will you be mine?

I can't stress how important it is for a couple to get to this point of leaving before cleaving. It's crucial for a couple to leave their family of origin to forge their own intimate union. I stress Genesis 2:24 in premarital counseling: "That is why a man leaves his father and mother and is united to his wife, and they become one flesh," a verse that is repeated nearly verbatim by Jesus in Matthew 19:5. You can't cleave to each other if you don't first leave. And your marriage won't be much of a fortress if a mother or father or mother-in-law or father-in-law can come between the two of you.

"A lot of things in our marriage have been hard, but there was never a question of whether we were a team," Janell says. "It was always the two of us."

If this has been a weak area in your marriage, have the painful conversation now and ask each other, *Have we emotionally and mentally left our families of origin to prioritize each other? Do you feel treasured and cherished above my parents and siblings? Or do you feel like you must compete with them or be subservient to their needs and wishes?*

After Garrett was born, Joe had to step in again and remind his mom that she needed to back off a bit. "She was a doting grand-mother and getting overly possessive of Garrett to the point of disregarding Janell as his mom." Holidays were filled with little jabs, particularly when Joe made the decision that they wouldn't be at his parents' house for every holiday (even though his siblings always were). Husbands, please note that Joe took the heat off Janell. He didn't leave his wife to fight this war on her own. "Leaving and cleaving" isn't usually a onetime decision; it has to become a policy.

So before their marriage suffered the huge shock of losing a child, Joe and Janell's fortress rested on two solid foundations: a passion for God and a commitment to leave their families so they could completely cleave to each other. They would need both of those foundations—and more, much more—in the days ahead.

AN EARLY CHALLENGE

As an infant, Garrett was "the easiest, greatest baby in the world." Janell wanted to get pregnant again immediately and never went back on birth control, hoping to have three or even four children, but she and Joe were never able to have more kids.

The struggle with infertility took a toll on their marriage. "It was emasculating for Joe, though the doctors said we were equally to blame for being unable to conceive." One of the things infertility does is to take what should be a delight—sexual intimacy—and turn it into a chore.

"Trying to conceive can take so much from your enjoyment of sexual intimacy," Janell says. "It eliminates it!" Joe adds. But it took more than a toll on their sexual intimacy; it had a huge impact on their marriage. Janell explains, "What it did to us emotionally was horrible. We both felt inadequate, and at various times we ended up blaming each other and fighting depression, and Joe even underwent surgery. It was one thing after another that took a large toll on us and our marriage."

Their struggle went on for several years, until Janell entered her forties. *Every month* brought another disappointment. "Even though we had this beautiful boy, not having more was like a hole in our home," says Janell.

When conflict arises, Joe is a "turtle" and Janell is a "tiger." As a trial lawyer, Joe fights raucous battles every day, so when he comes home, he just wants peace and at this point in their marriage refused to fight. Janell wanted to talk through the difficulties they were facing. Their opposing modes of dealing with conflict pushed them further apart. Physical intimacy became sporadic; they could go months without being sexually intimate.

Notice how one hit—in this case, the inability to conceive more children—set them up for another hit, emotional frustration, which set the table for a third hit: sex as a burden more than a blessing. Be vigilant about a *cascading distance* between the two of you. A physical challenge can become an emotional challenge, which can create a spiritual challenge or a relational challenge.

Perhaps because Garrett was their only child, they also fell prey to what every counselor says not to do: "We poured everything we had into Garrett to the detriment of our marriage."

Janell explains, "I'm not going to say we made him an idol, but he got a *lot* of attention."

The temptation was even greater because Garrett was "a great kid, a wonderful kid, with so many talents and gifts," Joe says. "He was the kind of child you look at and say, 'This kid just has it.'"

With a son to dote on; a demanding, stress-filled job to occupy Joe's day; and Janell's own business to run, they began mostly coexisting. They were heavily involved in church and looked fine (even strong) on the outside, but the walls of their marriage were thin.

THE AFFAIR

As Joe grew more distant from his wife, he grew closer in affection to a coworker, until eventually he began an emotional affair. It never became physical, but it was romantic.

> I quit talking to Janell because it was usually contentious, and I talked to my coworker. I felt affirmation from her that I did not get from Janell. Like many men, I felt like I needed affirmation and praise, and I didn't feel like I was getting it from Janell. Looking back, I was probably getting more than I thought I was, but it didn't feel like it.
>
> Since I'm usually very complimentary of people, I naturally spoke that way to my coworker, who took notice. "You always say the right things. You always know the right thing to do," she'd tell me.

The romantic infatuation continued for two years. Joe finally ended the emotional affair—without Janell finding out about it—in January 2012, about ten months before Garrett died. "It was my faith more than anything that led me to end it," Joe explains. "I knew it was wrong, and I told her we had to go back to being strictly professional in all our communication—no more texting and sweet-talking. She agreed."

While ending an emotional affair is an essential *first* step to putting your marriage back together, it doesn't on its own fix the marriage. Without any substantive change in their marriage and following a long stretch filled with many horrible turns of events (the life of a trial lawyer), Joe sent his coworker an intimate text once again in which he shared his feelings.

This time, he forgot to delete it from his phone, and Janell saw it.

Janell knew their marriage wasn't what it should be, but she thought Joe's faith would have prevented him from doing something like this. After a painful confrontation, they sought counseling individually and together.

"The counseling drew us closer and helped us hear each other's view about what was and wasn't going on in marriage," says Janell. They knew that if they didn't start working on their marriage, they were going to lose it.

A DIVINE DISCLOSURE

Here's a surprising twist in their story. Joe says, "I firmly believe that if Janell had not seen that text in May 2012, our marriage would never have survived the loss of our son. Between May and November 4, our relationship was renewed and strengthened more than it had been for years, so we were much more of a fortress when the blow came than we would have been if I had kept going back and forth with my coworker."

Here's primarily what changed to make them stronger.

1. *They began to pray more frequently individually and together.*

   "We had never prayed as much together as we should," says Joe. "Our daily walks with the Lord tended to be individual rather than joint. That changed as we worked to reestablish our marriage."

"Pray in the Spirit on all occasions with all kinds of prayers and requests." (Ephesians 6:18)

2. *They became more open with each other.*

Joe began talking more; Janell started listening more. They became more aware of each other's temptations, hurts, and desires. The walls between them began coming down.

"Confess your sins to each other and pray for each other so that you may be healed." (James 5:16)

3. *They strengthened their sexual and emotional connection.*

"Our increased connection in this way came from working on the other aspects of our marriage. I think we both felt more secure in the relationship and more comfortable with each other," says Janell.

4. *They became better friends.*

This friendship would be tested but prove strong on November 4, 2012.

NOVEMBER 4

The knock at the front door came at 6:30 a.m. Janell was already awake, drinking her coffee and sitting next to their beloved dogs. She had spent the previous day with Garrett in College Station. It was a moms weekend at Texas A&M, and Janell was scheduled to sing a solo at church Sunday morning, so she didn't stay in College Station, wanting to get back to Houston that night. She had left Garrett at about 10:00 p.m.

That morning, Janell heard a light tapping on the front door. She had slept in one of Joe's shirts and didn't have her usual pajamas or robe on, so she tiptoed to the door and could see through the shutters that a police car was parked sideways in their driveway.

"I knew instantly that Garrett was gone," she says.

Speaking through the glass, the policeman asked, "Are you Mrs. Luce?"

"Yes."

"Is your husband there?"

"Yes."

"Would you go get him?"

Janell ran upstairs, woke Joe up, and put on a robe.

"He was a very young police officer," Joe remembers. "I felt sorry for him. He didn't want to tell us what he had to tell us."

The officer held a piece of paper in his hands with a phone number. "I need you to call this number," he said.

Janell grabbed hold of his vest, turned him toward her so he had to look her in the eye, and said, "Just tell me, is our son dead?"

There was a brief hesitation. "Yes, ma'am."

"Do you have children?"

"Yes, ma'am, I do."

"Make sure you go home and hug them and tell them you love them."

The police officer was there for no more than five minutes. Joe called the College Station police department to get details. After drinking with his friends, Garrett had walked home early on the morning of November 4, leaving his truck in a parking lot. He fell down climbing up to some train tracks and was either knocked out or fell asleep on the train tracks, when an early-morning train came through College Station.

Janell and Garrett had enjoyed a nice dinner together just hours before his death. Garrett was nearly twenty years old, but he did occasionally binge drink. Joe and Janell had challenged him on this, and Janell became frustrated when, at the dinner, some of the moms were buying drinks for their sons.

Garrett had even asked Janell for a beer.

"Absolutely not! You're underage, and I am *not* providing you with alcohol. You know that."

Garrett laughed. "I know that," he said.

Some of the other moms invited Janell to stay and have a fun night out, but it bothered her that their attitude was along the lines of "Let's go out and party with our sons." She wasn't okay with that. Besides, she had to get up early to sing in Houston.

Of course, she wonders what might have happened had she stayed, but now she clings to the truth of Job 14:5: "A person's days are determined; you have decreed the number of his months and have set limits he cannot exceed."

"When I dropped him off, Garrett said, 'Mom, thanks so much for coming.'" He gave her a side hug in the car, and then before he got out, he came back and gave her a kiss on the cheek—something that was unusual for him to do.

When Janell got back to Houston, she got a text from Garrett: "Thanks for coming, Mom. I love you!"

Garrett's last physical act with his parents on this earth was to kiss Janell's cheek. His last communication was "I love you."

"One of the hardest things about Garrett's death," says Janell, "is that people might want to try to define him by his death.

Garrett was not a big partier. He was good looking, crazy intelligent, got top grades, tested well, had great people skills—the kind of kid who goes on to get an MBA at Harvard or Stanford. That's one of the hard things to think about in the wake of his death. It was so mind-numbingly dumb to drink to that level."

Joe is quick to turn the conversation to focus on God. "To us, Garrett is defined not by the remarkable way he died, but by the legacy of the great way God used him. He had never met a stranger and had a million best friends."

THE AFTERMATH

After the phone call with the College Station police, Janell turned on praise music. Joe made five phone calls to friends and church members, and then they got dressed. They prayed a simple prayer: "God, we have no clue how to handle this. Please help us." Loved ones began to stream into their house, their cars lining their block.

Janell pulled aside one of her closest friends and confided, "This situation is going to try to break my marriage. Statistically, there's a very good chance that this is what happens, and I need you to pray and help hold us together."

Initially, Janell admits that Joe was the strong one. "I come across as having a strong personality and being emotionally strong, but in that instance, I was not. I completely shut down. Joe was the epitome of strength and focus. He was crying, but he was present."

What gave Joe such strength? "You can't get through this unless the foundation is already laid," he said, "and I have based my life on the fact that God is God. I have proclaimed it in small

FACING A CATASTROPHIC LOSS

places and in front of five thousand people. I told myself, *If you can't stand on what you've been taught as a small child and tell others now, it doesn't count for much.*"

> "You, LORD, are my lamp;
>> the LORD turns my darkness into light.
> With your help I can advance against a troop;
>> with my God I can scale a wall."
>> (2 Samuel 22:29–30)

Possibly the strongest anchor for Joe's soul was, and still is, Paul's great declaration in Romans 8:31–39. Joe applies it this way: "When you are at the end of yourself, knowing that nothing in heaven or on earth can separate you from the love, peace, strength, compassion, and presence of Almighty God, that's a pretty good place from which to start your journey back."

For the next twelve months, Joe and Janell were, as Janell says, "stronger than ever, unified, on the same page. We cried and prayed together."

But after the one-year anniversary of Garrett's death, Joe's support group started evaporating. "We had our village of twenty to thirty couples," Joe explains, "who have been through so much of life together: car wrecks, surgeries, financial calamities. All these friends showed up en masse when Garrett died." But about a year afterward, a lot of Joe's support had disappeared, and most of his friends had stopped asking how he was doing.

"I had girlfriends watching out for me and Bible studies to keep me focused," Janell explains. "Not a day went by when I didn't get at least five encouraging text messages. That didn't stop for me at year one, but it did for Joe."

"We learned that year two is typically worse than year one," Janell says. "The first year is the year of all the firsts, and you're in a fog of trauma, just trying to survive. By the second year, the numbness has worn off, and all the pain is felt in a fresh way."

"Reality sets in," Joe explains.

Catastrophic loss goes well beyond the death of a child. Take, for example, Miriam and Caleb, who both felt chills when their son's psychiatrist referred to his "mental illness." It was one thing to admit he was difficult, but *mentally ill?* The first year, they researched options, got him into a treatment plan (which he quit), got him on medication (which he often stopped taking)—everything they could think of to help him thrive. By year two, the weariness of dealing with a son who sometimes called them more than fifty times a day to rant and rave (until they turned their phones off) began to wear on them. It's one thing to hear and accept a diagnosis; it's another thing altogether to learn how to live with it long-term.

To add to the hardship in Joe and Janell's life, Joe's work became more stressful as he worked on an explosive case. Following Garrett's death, Joe had responded to the stress by drinking coffee and walking up and down the hallway at work to tell "Garrett stories." But when he wound up being the lead attorney on a trial case with some unethical opponents, there was little time to grieve. In fact, his colleagues subtly (or not so subtly) demanded that he step up and support everyone else.

"We were surrounded by unprofessional lawyers, and I became the only guy everyone could talk to, which is crazy when I look back on it, since I was the emotional cripple whose son had died."

Joe confesses, "I can't describe the emotional, mental, professional, and even physical disaster this case was. I made a boatload of money, but it took so much out of me, I'm not sure it was worth it."

Janell concurs. "The greed, evil, lies, and cheating were like some kind of dark, swirling thing pulling him—and us—under."

It's important to note that making your marriage a fortress may mean facing *multiple* attacks at the same time. Rarely does a marriage have the luxury of focusing on just one issue. Our God is capable of helping us fight on many fronts, however: "For the LORD your God is the one who goes with you to fight for you against your *enemies* [plural] to give you victory" (Deuteronomy 20:4, emphasis added).

The ensuing stress led to an eruption on the Monday after Easter in 2014—about eighteen months after Garrett died—when Joe and Janell had a "yelling, screaming fight." True to his "turtle" nature, Joe walked out the door.

Janell was terrified. "I wasn't sure if he would drive himself off a bridge or just not come back." She called some of his friends and said, "Y'all gotta go get him; he needs help. He hasn't fully healed yet, and this case at work just put him over the edge."

Joe started intensive counseling, including addressing PTSD.

And that's when Janell became the strong one, largely because she needed to be. "Joe had nothing. He was empty."

The strongest marriages are the merger of two strong individuals. "Two are better than one, because they have a good return for their labor: If either of them falls down, one can help the other up" (Ecclesiastes 4:9–10). To make your marriage a fortress requires trying to become a fortress on your own, for the simple reason that over the course of a marriage, both partners will occasionally need to find shelter in the other. Joe explains, "I had to be willing to admit that Janell was wiser and smarter. I had to learn that wisdom and insight don't always flow through the husband."

Trials can increase a husband's love for his wife and a wife's love for her husband when each leans on the other and discovers that their partner is the very refuge they need. But this required Janell to be the strong woman she had worked for decades to become through studying God's Word and growing in prayer.

Joe's counselor told him that marital counseling wouldn't do much for him right then because his emotional reserves were empty. "You've got to deal with the PTSD and then get back into marital counseling."

Joe had to deal with his trauma before he could deal with his marriage. Fortunately, Janell was strong enough to wait.

Janell explains, "Marriage isn't always 50-50; sometimes it's 95-5. Immediately after Garrett's death, our marriage depended 95 percent on Joe and 5 percent on me; eighteen months later, it was 75 percent on me and 25 percent on Joe. You can't define your marriage by any one season, and you need to be willing to step up and be the sacrificial one, or at least the strong one, at various times."

Joe realized he had allowed the lawsuit to become his mental escape. When he came home to Janell, he told her, "When I look at you, I just see the face of my pain. Garrett looked so much like you that sometimes it just breaks my heart to see that resemblance."

For the next year, Joe and Janell had to work hard to keep pursuing honesty, to process their grief, and to learn how to stay together.

LESSONS LEARNED

Joe and Janell are proof that your marriage can survive some of life's most vicious assaults. Here are some tips they learned along the way.

UNDERSTAND YOU'RE BOTH GRIEVING IN DIFFERENT WAYS

A catastrophic loss changes you, but *it changes you differently than it changes your spouse*. Your spouse is going through a similar, but in another sense completely different, transformation. A mother's grief and a father's grief are both just as deep, but they are different.

Joe sought refuge in an incredibly challenging vocational task. He couldn't afford to stop and think. Janell had her worship music and friends to help her process her grief. Hers was definitely a healthier approach in the long term, but what really helped Janell was finally realizing why Joe was hesitant to come home to her. When he explained that her face reminded him of the son he had lost and that it was difficult to reconcile past loss and current devotion, Janell reached a new level of empathy and understanding.

ACCEPT THE FACT THAT TIME DOESN'T HEAL ALL WOUNDS

When you face a catastrophic loss, you're not just experiencing grief; you're experiencing trauma. And medically speaking, trauma takes a long time (and usually professional counseling) to heal from. Remember Miriam and Caleb? If you could have seen their faces as they left their son's psychiatrist following the mental illness diagnosis, you wouldn't just see sadness; you'd see *trauma*.

There's no shame in asking a doctor to take out your appendix instead of doing it yourself, and there's no shame in asking a licensed counselor to help you process trauma. Joe couldn't cure his PTSD with prayer and Bible study any more than someone can bring down their cholesterol by memorizing Psalm 23. One of the most loving things I can do as a pastor is to point hurting, wounded people to professional medical (including psychiatric) care. A couple will occasionally come to me with multiple issues in their lives and marriage and ask me to recommend a licensed marriage counselor. But by now, I know some issues are best dealt with individually before couples counseling commences. You can't have a strong marriage with a seriously weak spouse. Trauma is a wound to your psyche that is every bit as serious as a hernia, internal bleeding, or something similar that you can't just wish away or heal on your own. Whether the traumatic injury was sexual abuse, the tragic loss of a parent, extensive bullying, or something else, it's not dishonoring to God to say that prayer isn't enough to deal with it.

Janell cautions couples, "When you lose a child, the pain does not go away. Time does not heal. What happens is you become stronger and you learn how to live with the hole and live with the pain and hopefully develop the emotional strength to help others. But even years later, there will be times of overwhelming grief when you just need to cry."

Remember Billy and Emma from chapter 7? They still feel an ache when they drive by the neighborhood where they used to live and are reminded of the beloved home they had to sell.

Professional licensed counseling can provide tools to process your hurt and help you develop inner strength, as well as offer strategies to face anxiety, depression, manic episodes, or panic attacks when they hit.

Janell goes on, "The pain is *always* there, and it's just as intense today as it was eight years ago. *Garrett is still not here!* But I am so much stronger today than I was then, and so I can cope with the loss and rest in the hope that we will see him again."

Expecting the emotional crash and a new onslaught of grief after your numbness wears off is a wise thing to do. For Joe and Janell, the trauma began to resurface after the first anniversary of Garrett's death. It overwhelmed Joe about eighteen months after Garrett's passing. The timeline may well be different for you, but don't be caught by surprise. This is a normal pattern that grief follows.

Every time one of Garrett's friends gets married, gets hired, or becomes a father, the Luces are reminded not only of what they have lost but of what they are losing. There's no getting around it—but that reality has led to one of the most astonishing expressions of faith I've ever heard a couple utter, which I'll share in a moment.

FIGHT BITTERNESS WITH GRATITUDE

An early church father named Ambrose lost a beloved brother who was his closest earthly companion. In his reflections on his brother's death, he said something particularly memorable: "To this must be added that I cannot be ungrateful to God; for I must rather rejoice that I had such a brother than grieve that I had lost a brother, for the former is a gift, the latter a debt to be paid."[52]

Craig and Sheri, a married couple who lost a toddler, found healing and comfort in choosing to be thankful to God for his sovereignty in life and death:

> Be thankful for the time you had with your precious one, rather than bitter or angry about the time that won't be there.

What is a life? For some, it is 70 years, or 80 years or 90 years. But for Velissa, it was about two years and 10 months. That was her life . . . There is nowhere we are told life should be "X" years long. To the Lord, a thousand years is like unto a day and a day like a thousand years. Time is not a problem to the Lord.[53]

Joe and Janell celebrate the two wonderful decades that Garrett had with them. He had influenced many young people. He was a son to be proud of. They had enjoyed many wonderful times together, watching him play ball and spiritually encourage younger boys. They are as grateful for what they had as they are sad for what they've lost.

MAINTAIN YOUR FAITH

Joe and Janell don't pretend they've overcome this challenge and therefore don't need to keep building their marriage. They have read through the entire Bible for three out of the four years following Garrett's death.

"Something new always stands out," Joe says. They couldn't make the grief go away, but they could allow God's Word to come in and speak God's message to them. As the psalmist promises, "Your word is a lamp for my feet, a light on my path" (Psalm 119:105). Joe explains:

We have sought to live out our faith in the full expression of all that it means: singing and dancing, teaching classes, being a deacon, being a choir mom, cooking hamburgers for outreach events—whatever the church needs.

In the end, there was no question of where our strength came from. Because of all those years from when I became a Christian at seven and Janell gave her heart to Jesus at thirteen, everything that God had poured into us came into fruition and strengthened us. We don't know what new challenges we'll face in the future, but we want to keep growing in the Lord and growing our marriage to face them.

TAKE HOLD OF THE HOPE OF HEAVEN

This is the part of Joe and Janell's story that inspired me so much. They have a profound theological understanding of the hope of heaven and have applied it to their loss. "God didn't just take Garrett *from* us," Janell told me with deep conviction. "He called Garrett *to* something. It is God's will that Garrett is in heaven this day. I believe that Garret Luce is fulfilling his heavenly calling in a glorious way."

I teared up thinking about this application of faith. The real promise of heaven—to be "away from the body" is to be "at home with the Lord" (2 Corinthians 5:8)—holds Joe and Janell up so strongly that, in one sense, they can see even the *benefits* of Garrett's death. This is one of the most astonishing expressions of faith I've ever heard. Janell says:

I don't have to deal with a difficult daughter-in-law or the other issues that can arise for parents of adult kids. I've seen how some of my friends struggle over the problems faced by their adult children—the poor choices they make, struggling marriages, serious health concerns over their grandchildren. Some watch adult children become dependent on alcohol or get divorced.

I will never have to deal with that pain. Instead, I get to imagine the glorious things that Garrett is doing in heaven *right now.* He is fulfilling God's purpose for him in the heavenly realm in a perfect and wonderful way. And yes, I believe he is watching me, telling other saints, "That's my mom. I told you she is strong." I still want to make him proud of me.

The Lord is sovereign. He is good, and he has a plan. Garrett is perfectly fulfilling that plan.

My jaw dropped open at this declaration of faith. Joe saw my astonishment and added his thoughts:

We've been told a thousand times, "Oh, you have such great faith, such strong faith." That's not true. We have desperate faith. But this desperate faith has grown and matured.

You have to make a choice. We could crawl into our closet where no light can get in, or we can choose to stand. In marriage it's the same thing. You have to make the choice. You have to choose to reclaim it and participate in it and grow it. We're the epitome of Paul's mystery that all things work together for good.

For couples still striving to make the choice of giving in or persevering, Janell counsels, "Your grief will bring you into the fog, but the Holy Spirit is present in that fog. Keep your mind and ears open. I heard songs and Bible verses I needed to hear. Some days it was like I was bombarded with holy missives of help. Just keep your ears and eyes open, and God will bring you what you need. If a couple will just lean into the fog, they'll find that the Holy Spirit is present in the fog."

Embrace the reality mentioned by Paul: "Praise be to the God and Father of our Lord Jesus Christ, the Father of compassion and the God of all comfort, who comforts us in all our troubles, so that we can comfort those in any trouble with the comfort we ourselves receive from God" (2 Corinthians 1:3–4).

DIVINE PREPARATION

Finally, Joe and Janell also see God's kindness in preparing them for what was about to happen. God is sovereign (see Deuteronomy 3:24; 2 Samuel 7:22), and he prepared this couple ahead of time. For instance, they had moved to a new house just before Garrett went to work at a summer camp and then left for school in the fall, so he never really lived with them in that house. They didn't have to process the "memories of space" that can bring deep pain to so many who have lost loved ones, such as remembering Garrett sitting in his favorite corner, watching a game on that couch, or laughing with his friends in that kitchen.*

Joe and Janell's new house also had a massive master suite that became their refuge as their new home filled up with comforters and mourners. "Prior to Garrett's death," says Janell, "it also served as sort of a honeymoon suite that was new and fresh and allowed us to reconnect spiritually, physically, and emotionally before Garrett died so that when he did die, we were in a place of renewal."

Because they'd had to work through Joe's emotional affair, they were reading books, pursuing reconciliation, and growing

---

* Of course, many couples find such space memories comforting. Every couple, and every individual, grieves and heals in their own way.

toward each other with a new determination. "We thought we were saving our marriage because of the emotional affair; we didn't realize something even bigger than the emotional affair was coming up."

The divine nature of Janell's discovery—especially considering that Joe had covered up the affair for almost two years—leads to the conclusion that God knew it was time for Joe and Janell to get healed and to get strong and to become a fortress for the assault that was approaching. He shepherded them into a place of safety before the wolf could attack. I've talked to other couples who thank God that they joined a new church or got into a new Bible study (and one man who was especially thankful for a new job with healthy coworkers) months before an attack hit. God is a creative God who has many ways and means of preparing us for what's ahead.

One of the lessons I pray you'll take away from this book is to realize you're not the only one trying to make your marriage a fortress. God is leading you, guiding you, and preparing you. Think of these familiar words from Psalm 23 in that light:*

> The LORD is our shepherd, we lack nothing.
> He makes us lie down in green pastures,
> he leads us beside quiet waters,
> he refreshes our souls.
> He guides us along the right paths
> for his name's sake.
> Even though we walk
> through the darkest valley,

---

* I've taken the liberty of putting in plural references where the psalmist David speaks only of himself.

we will fear no evil,
>   for you are with us;
> your rod and your staff,
>   they comfort us.

Joe and Janell's Good Shepherd had guided them to a place of rest and comfort and nourishment, so that when they had to walk through the darkest valley, they had what they needed to survive.

"The months leading up to Garrett's death were some of the happiest Joe and I had ever shared. We were a different couple when Garrett came home at the end of the summer than when he left. "Y'all weren't much fun to be around before I left," he had told us, "but now it's embarrassing in a whole different way."

They both treasure the thought that Garrett's last view of them was as a loving, supportive, fun, and even flirty couple. One year before, their walls were broken, the foundations were shaking, the roof was threatening to collapse. But under God's shepherding care, when the worst assault of their life hit, their marriage was a fortress of strength and stood strong as Joe and Janell faced their grief hand in hand and heart to heart.

> But I will sing of your strength,
>   in the morning I will sing of your love;
> for you are my fortress,
>   my refuge in times of trouble.
>
> You are my strength, I sing praise to you;
>   you, God, are my fortress,
>   my God on whom I can rely. (Psalm 59:16–17)

239

::

Building Your Fortress Takeaways

1. Growing deeper in your walk with Christ through consistent worship, prayer, and Bible study can prepare you for catastrophic heartbreak before the heartbreak even happens. To get and stay close to your spouse, focus first on getting and staying close to your God.

2. To survive a crisis, couples need to be a strong team, which means leaving your family of origin and cleaving to each other. Leaving isn't usually a onetime decision. It has to become a policy.

3. If you feel distant in your relationship, work hard to be more open, to connect more, and to become better friends. These investments will help you be strong enough to face catastrophic loss.

4. The second year is often more difficult than the first year when a couple suffers tragic loss.

5. Making your marriage a fortress sometimes means facing multiple attacks at the same time. Rarely does a marriage have the luxury of focusing on just one issue.

6. Because individuals grieve differently, one spouse may be strong when the other is weak, and vice versa.

7. You may need to deal with individual trauma before marital counseling proves fruitful.

8. Trauma usually requires professional care to heal. Time won't make it go away on its own.

::

9. Spiritually, it helps to be grateful for what you had instead of focusing only on what you've lost.

10. Cling to the hope of heaven.

11. Remember that the Holy Spirit is preparing you to face your trials, helping you get through them, and comforting you in the aftermath. We do not face any trial alone.

CHAPTER 10

· · · · · · · · · · · · · · · ·

GOING FORWARD

Fortifying Your Marriage with
a Deeper Spiritual Connection

Les and Leslie are bestselling authors of numerous Christian books on marriage, sought-after speakers, and relationship experts. They live in Seattle, but their travels have taken them all over the world. The state of Oklahoma employed them for a year to bring down the divorce rate in their state (it worked, by the way). And their teachings and writings have blessed millions.

In spite of their psychological training and Christian upbringing, for many years in their marriage one thing was missing—a shared spiritual intimacy. They had individual spiritual intimacy, but they never thought to intentionally build it together. Their marriage went to a new level when they sought what they call "the oneness that only a shared commitment to spiritual discovery can bring."[54]

Unlike the other chapters in this book, this one doesn't focus on a couple's problem but rather on a couple's solution. The reason is that spiritual intimacy is a remedy (not necessarily a cure, but certainly some help) for *every* situation. Getting closer to God prepares us to face any problem life can throw our way.

One of the great challenges in building spiritual intimacy is our pride. We think our way of loving God is the best (and sometimes even the *only*) way. When Lisa and I were in college, I got up early to pray because that's what Jesus did (see Mark 1:35). Lisa rolled out of bed just early enough to comb her hair and get to her first class. She postponed her quiet time until after lunch, when she would go to the dorm roof, stretch out in the sun with her Bible, and have her time with the Lord.

In the flirty way that interested college students do, I teased Lisa. "Come on," I asked her, "who goes up onto the roof after lunch and calls that a 'quiet time'?" A few weeks later, I heard a knock on my dorm room door. I opened it, and a smiling Lisa walked in, went over to my desk, and opened my Bible to Acts 10:9: "About noon the following day . . . Peter went up on the roof to pray."

It was funny and instructive. And it was the first of several life experiences that God used to lead me to be less rigid about how people connect with him.

That eventually led to my writing the book *Sacred Pathways: Nine Ways to Connect with God*. In it, I lay out nine "sacred pathways" or spiritual temperaments that are revealed in Scripture and church history. Understanding how your spouse loves God and wants to spend time with God is one of the most important intimacy-building things you can know about them, so I'm going to give a short summary of each pathway. See if you can recognize where you and your spouse line up.

1. **THE NATURALIST.** Naturalists are those believers whose hearts most awaken to God when they get outside and are surrounded by all that he has made. Being surrounded by God's creation bends naturalists toward worship and adoration. Trying to pray inside a room with their heads bowed and eyes closed would be one of the least effective prayer styles for them.

2. **THE SENSATE.** The best avenues for some believers to commune with God are the five senses—tasting, touching, hearing, seeing, and even smelling. Just as naturalists are spiritually awakened while walking through a forest, so sensates become spiritually attuned when their senses are brought into play. Majestic music, symbolic architecture, outstanding art, or the sensory experience of communion are dear friends and powerful spiritual aids.

3. **THE TRADITIONALIST.** For traditionalists, religion isn't a dirty word; it is an outgrowth of their relationship with God. These believers appreciate the role of ritual, which builds on the power of reinforced behavior. There is something profound for them in worshiping God according to set patterns—their own, or history's. They may organize their life around scheduled times of prayer and may even choose to carefully observe the Christian calendar, aligning themselves with centuries of faith. In addition to establishing rituals, traditionalists often make good use of Christian symbols. And while routine can be boring to some and spiritually soporific for others, for the traditionalist the familiar patterns of worship can function like a high-powered battery lighting up the reality of God's presence.

4. **THE ASCETIC.** When you think of an ascetic, think of a monk or nun. Ascetics meet God internally. They don't want the distractions of a museum or a group meeting. They prefer to shut out the world and meet God in solitude and austerity. For them, the best environment for personal worship is silence, without any noise or colorful stimulants. Accordingly, ascetics usually need to get alone on a regular basis. They may prefer solitary retreats or at least a quiet place with a rather orderly environment. They are often advocates of all-night prayer vigils and many of the classic disciplines, such as fasting and meditation. Please don't take it personally if your spouse is an ascetic and needs some time alone to best connect with God. You and your marriage will be immensely blessed if you encourage your spouse to connect with God rather than getting in the way or resenting it.

5. **THE ACTIVIST.** Activists love to meet God in the vortex of confrontation. They want to fight God's battles. For them, church is primarily a place to collect signatures and recruit volunteers for the "real work" of the gospel, which takes place outside the church building.

6. **THE CAREGIVER.** Caregivers love God by loving others. Providing care and meeting needs in Jesus' name spiritually energizes them and draws them ever closer to the Lord. For caregivers, caregiving isn't an obligation so much as a threshold to intimacy with God. Caregiving extends beyond nursing sick people; it can include fixing a widow's car, serving as a volunteer firefighter, or researching a cure for a disease.

7. **THE ENTHUSIAST.** An enthusiast loves the excitement and celebration of their faith. They tend to be more relational and

therefore may favor group worship as they feed off the excitement of other believers praising God. Enthusiasts also revel in God's mystery and supernatural power. They like to take spiritual risks and wake up hoping that God will do something new and fresh. Enthusiasts don't just want to know scriptural concepts; they want to experience and be moved by them. Their exuberance tends to lead them to embrace things like dancing, music, drawing, singing, and other creative forms of worship.

8. **THE CONTEMPLATIVE.** Contemplatives are marked by an emotional attachment and even abandonment to God. They are God's lovers, and they want to spend their time in God's presence, adoring him, listening to him, and simply enjoying him. Contemplatives enjoy doing the things couples like to do—demonstrating their love for God through secret acts of devotion, giving gifts to God like the gift of a poem, or doing anonymous acts of charity. They often favor the discipline of journal writing in which they can explore their heart's devotion.

9. **THE INTELLECTUAL.** In this context, intellectual doesn't necessarily mean "smart" but rather a heart that is most often awakened when they understand new concepts about God. Their minds are very active, and new intellectual understanding births affection; it creates respect for the Creator, which leads to worship. Just as the naturalist can't wait to get out of doors, the sensate is eager to visit the cathedral, and the ascetic scurries off into their inner world, so the intellectual seeks God in the pages of a book, an inspiring lecture or sermon, or the vast ruminations of their minds.

MOST OF US ARE BLENDS

Do you see yourself in any of the above categories? Don't feel that you have to choose just one. Most of us are blends, and many of us will move in and out of certain temperaments as we age. The important thing is not to find the right label but to understand how you and your spouse best connect with God so you can more deliberately and consciously cultivate an increasing affection for your Creator.* As you've read in the previous chapters, the most common element for couples to grow through various challenges is the deepening of their spiritual roots.

LES AND LESLIE

Les and Leslie warn, "One of the single biggest stumbling blocks to spiritual intimacy in a marriage is a failure to understand and appreciate the other's spiritual language. In other words, if we don't recognize that our partner's means of communion with God is valid, we discount it. Intentionally or not, we send a message to our partner that says *you don't know God like I do.*"[55]

Leslie is the classic contemplative. "I like nothing more than to spend a couple hours each day alone with God. Having a toddler at my feet has put a crimp in my style, but this still remains my primary pathway to God. I have had the same prayer book for years and the same well-worn Bible too. They keep me company as I seek to love God with the purest and deepest love I can."[56]

---

* My book *Sacred Pathways* (1996; Grand Rapids: Zondervan, 2020) examines each temperament much more thoroughly, with tests and information about each temperament's particular temptations.

Les is the classic intellectual. "I feel closest to God when I am learning a new truth. If I can conceptualize some aspect of the Christian life in a new or fresh way, if I can wrap my mind around a truth, I come alive in my relationship with God. The time I most often spend with God is while I'm reading a new book or working in my study, lined with reference tools that help me in my spiritual pursuit."[57]

Before they read *Sacred Pathways*, Leslie viewed Les's approach as "too academic and emotionally removed," and both of them expected "the other to conform more to our individual leanings."[58] But now they seek to join their pathways rather than compete with each other in their pathways.

> I (Leslie) am not expecting Les to wake early so he can enjoy a quiet time with me; in fact, I'm learning how invigorating it can be to study a topic with Les in one of his commentaries. And I (Les) am learning the profound stirring in my heart that comes from a contemplative moment of doing nothing more than being with God. We are not converting each other to fit into a style that is not natural, but we are encouraging each other's means to God like we have never done in the past.[59]

To prepare for, get through, and recover from life's assaults, sink your roots deeper into the soil of intimacy with God. Talk through the pathways (or slowly read through *Sacred Pathways* together to discover your pathway) to gain new understanding and appreciation of your spouse. Then explore how you can encourage each other to draw closer to God.

The theme of my ministry has been "Closer to Christ, Closer to Others." Marriage reaches its pinnacle when we allow our desire to be closer to each other to lead us to a closer walk with God, which helps us to love each other more, which casts us into further dependence on God, creating a glorious circle of love and faith. I believe it is the life all of us are meant to live.

You make your marriage a fortress by making your soul a fortress of devotion and surrender to God. When the two of you combine your devotion, your marriage will become even stronger.

> Let all the faithful pray to you
> while you may be found;
> surely the rising of the mighty waters
> will not reach them. (Psalm 32:6)

Building Your Fortress Takeaways

1. A shared commitment to spiritual discovery can strengthen your marriage.
2. Getting closer to God strengthens us individually and as a couple and helps prepare us for any kind of challenge we may face along the way.
3. Pridefully assuming that our way of relating to God is better than our spouse's frustrates spiritual intimacy.
4. Understanding how your spouse loves God and wants to spend time with God is one of the most important intimacy-building things you can know about them.

5. The nine sacred pathways are naturalists, sensates, tra-ditionalists, ascetics, activists, caregivers, enthusiasts, contemplatives, and intellectuals.

6. When it comes to the pathways, most of us are blends, and many of us will move in and out of certain pathways as we age.

7. Drs. Les and Leslie Parrott believe that "one of the single biggest stumbling blocks to spiritual intimacy in a marriage is a failure to understand and appreciate the other's spiritual language . . . If we don't recognize that our partner's means of communion with God is valid, we discount it."

8. Instead of trying to convert your spouse into your style of relating to God or judging your spouse's style, try to understand and learn from their style.

9. Marriage reaches its pinnacle when we allow our desire to be closer to each other to lead us to a closer walk with God, which helps us to love each other more, which casts us into further dependence on God, creating a glorious circle of love and faith.

ACKNOWLEDGMENTS

I'd like to thank my editor Andy Rogers for pushing me to hone the message of this book and make it even more applicable to more couples. Dirk Buursma once again did a wonderful job with the manuscript editing. To Webster Younce and Paul Fisher at Zondervan—thanks for your partnership in this work.

Lisa Thomas, Rebekah Taylor, Bonny Burns, Dr. Jake Porter, Tim Mavergeorge, Dr. Steve Wilke, and Mary Kay Smith all read earlier portions of this manuscript and provided helpful feedback.

To my agents Curtis Yates and Mike Salisbury at Yates and Yates—I can't imagine doing this without you. And to Alli Sepulveda—I'm so grateful that you've joined the team full-time. To Mark Sepulveda—your friendship and support are so helpful.

Finally, in the sometimes crazy world of evangelical publishing, it's a particular gift to have some special "writer friends" who help keep me sane and enjoying the process. To Ted Cunningham, Shaunti Feldhahn, and Les Parrott—thanks for the group texts (sometimes funny, sometimes serious, sometimes just really sad) and phone calls and for your partnership in marriage ministry.

NOTES

1. John Owen, *The Works of John Owen* (Edinburgh: Johnstone and Hunter, 1851), 6:132.
2. Teresa of Ávila, *The Interior Castle*, in *The Collected Works of Teresa of Ávila*, trans. Kieran Kavanaugh and Otilio Rodriguez (Washington, DC: Institute of Carmelite Studies Publications, 1980), 291–92.
3. D. A. Carson, *How Long, O Lord? Reflections on Suffering and Evil*, 2nd ed. (Grand Rapids: Baker Academic, 2006), 67.
4. See Esther Fleece, *No More Faking Fine: Ending the Pretending* (Grand Rapids: Zondervan, 2017), 38. I heartily recommend this book for its helpful insights into grieving.
5. Les and Leslie Parrott, *I Love You More: How Everyday Problems Can Strengthen Your Marriage* (Grand Rapids: Zondervan, 2005), 63.
6. Archibald Hart and Sharon May, *Safe Haven Marriage: Building a Relationship You Want to Come Home To* (Nashville: W Publishing, 2003), 8.
7. Parrotts, *I Love You More*, 78.
8. Hart and May, *Safe Haven Marriage*, 9.
9. Much of my discussion about withdrawal is based on Hart and May, *Safe Haven Marriage*, 101–2; see also Ellie Lisitsa, "The Four Horsemen: Stonewalling," Gottman Institute, www.gottman.com/blog/the-four -horsemen-stonewalling.
10. Cited in Hart and May, *Safe Haven Marriage*, 102.
11. Cited in Hart and May, *Safe Haven Marriage*, 104.
12. Hart and May, *Safe Haven Marriage*, 15–16, italics in original.
13. Gordon D. Fee, *The First Epistle to the Corinthians*, New International Commentary on the New Testament (Grand Rapids: Eerdmans, 1987), 205.

14. Gordon Fee, *God's Empowering Presence: The Holy Spirit in the Letters of Paul* (1994; repr., Grand Rapids: Baker Academic, 2011), 124.

15. Rob and Joanna Teigen, "Podcast Episode 7: How to Stay Connected as a Couple When You Have to Be Apart," *Growing Home Together* podcast, September 29, 2020, https://growinghometogether.com/podcast-episode -7-how-to-stay-connected-as-a-couple-when-you-have-to-be-apart.

16. See Joy P. Skarka, "Sexual Shame in Women and How to Experience Freedom," DEdMin diss. (Dallas Theological Seminary, 2021).

17. Gary L. Thomas, *Devotions for a Sacred Marriage: A Year of Weekly Devotions for Couples* (Grand Rapids: Zondervan, 2005).

18. Teigens, "Podcast Episode 7: How to Stay Connected," *Growing Home Together* podcast.

19. Hart and May, *Safe Haven Marriage*, 29.

20. For Hart and May's lengthier and more professional description (I'm summarizing their thoughts here), see chapter 3 of *Safe Haven Marriage*, 27–46.

21. Hart and May, *Safe Haven Marriage*, 7.

22. Hart and May, *Safe Haven Marriage*, 19.

23. For more on David and Terri's adventure-based marriage retreats, visit their website at www.marriagelifeministries.com.

24. As an ardent believer that the 1970s produced the greatest decade of music *ever*, I heartily concur with David's advice. How can you not fall in love with your spouse again while listening to "You Light Up My Life" by Debby Boone, "You Are the Woman" by Firefall, "Still the One" by Orleans, "More Than a Woman" by the Bee Gees, "All I Know" by Art Garfunkel, "Always and Forever" by Heatwave, "Beautiful" by Gordon Lightfoot, "I Go Crazy" by Paul Davis, "I'll Stand by You" by the Pretenders, "The Lady in Red" by Chris de Burgh, "Lovin' You" by Minnie Riperton, "She's Always a Woman" by Billy Joel, "Sometimes When We Touch" by Dan Hill, "Wonderful Tonight" by Eric Clapton, "You Are So Beautiful" by Joe Cocker, "You Are the Sunshine of My Life" by Stevie Wonder, "You're in My Heart" by Rod Stewart, and "Let's Stay Together" by Al Green? If you ever see me in person, I can share so many more! And if you want to get romantic, there's "Let's Get It On" by Marvin Gaye, "Right Time of the Night" by Jennifer Warnes, and just about anything by Barry White.

25. Parrotts, *I Love You More*, 44.

26. Parrotts, *I Love You More*, 46, italics in original.

27. For an excellent book on improving our listening skills, see Klaus Bockmuehl, *Listening to the God Who Speaks: Reflections on God's Guidance from Scripture and the Lives of God's People* (Colorado Springs: Helmers & Howard, 1990).

28. See Matthew 7:3–5.

29. Les and Leslie Parrott have written a fabulous book on empathy titled *Trading Places: The Best Move You'll Ever Make in Your Marriage* (Grand Rapids: Zondervan, 2008).

30. There's a big difference between distraction and destruction. Busyness that results in apathy is one thing. It still needs to be addressed, but busyness that results in abusive behavior goes beyond being a marital issue and requires defense. I talk about this in my book *When to Walk Away: Finding Freedom from Toxic People* (Grand Rapids: Zondervan, 2019).

31. Parrotts, *I Love You More*, 123.

32. Hart and May, *Safe Haven Marriage*, 16, italics in original.

33. Remember here that I'm referring to mutual submission as an expression of intimacy, not of domineering or abusive behavior. It's one thing for a wife to be uncomfortable with a husband who connects with old flames on Facebook; it's another thing if one spouse is controlling and demanding to be a gatekeeper for every connection in a threatening and oppressive way. See my book *When to Walk Away* for a more thorough discussion of this.

34. See 2 Kings 5:1–14.

35. Check out my and Debra Fileta's book *Married Sex: A Christian Couple's Guide to Reimagining Your Love Life* (Grand Rapids: Zondervan, 2021).

36. Thomas and Fileta, *Married Sex*.

37. Cited in HealthyWomen Editors, "What's the Key to Female Orgasm during Sex?" HealthyWomen, April 22, 2016, www.healthywomen.org/content/article/whats-key-female-orgasm-during-sex. See also Kim Wallen and Elisabeth Lloyd, "Female Sexual Arousal: Genital Anatomy and Orgasm in Intercourse," *Hormones and Behavior* 59, no. 5 (May 2011): 780-92, www.sciencedirect.com/science/article/abs/pii/S0018506X10002990?via%3Dihub.

38. Quotes in this paragraph are from "20: Dealing with Desire Level Differences with Jessa Zimmerman," *Get Your Marriage On! with Dan Purcell* podcast, https://getyourmarriageon.com/20-dealing-with-desire-level-differences-with-jessa-zimmerman.

39. According to EMDR.com (www.emdr.com/what-is-emdr), "Eye

Movement Desensitization and Reprocessing (EMDR) is a psychotherapy treatment that was originally designed to alleviate the distress associated with traumatic memories."

40. Jessica Dickler, "Being Rich May Increase Your Odds of Divorce," CNBC, October 10, 2018, www.cnbc.com/2018/10/10/being-rich-may-increase -your-odds-of-divorce.html.

41. Markus Barth, *Ephesians 4–6*, Anchor Bible (Garden City, NY: Doubleday, 1974), 514.

42. See Exodus 32:19; Numbers 20:11–12.

43. Tom Wright, *Paul for Everyone: The Prison Letters* (Louisville, KY: Westminster John Knox, 2004), 55.

44. Gary Thomas and Drs. Steve and Rebecca Wilke, *Nine Essential Conversations Before You Say I Do* (Colorado Springs: Cook, 2021).

45. Stormie Omartian, *The Power of a Praying Wife* (Eugene, OR: Harvest House, 1997).

46. Frank Viola, *Hang On, Let Go: What to Do When Your Dreams Are Shattered and Life Is Falling Apart* (Carol Stream, IL: Tyndale Momentum, 2021), 318–21.

47. The *Diagnostic and Statistical Manual of Mental Disorders* (DSM-5) doesn't list "sexual addiction" as a mental disorder. Whether it should be included is part of an ongoing debate. It goes beyond my expertise to argue one way or another, but Robert Weiss has written a piece explaining why he thinks it should be included. See Robert Weiss, "New Research Supports Sexual Addiction as a Legitimate Diagnosis," American Addiction Centers, November 4, 2019, https://rehabs.com/pro -talk/new-research-supports-sexual-addiction-as-a-legitimate-diagnosis.

48. Quotes from Dr. Porter are taken from private communications, verbally or in writing, after he read an early draft of this chapter.

49. If lying is a challenge, it can be helpful to understand *why* you lie. Dr. Michael Johnson has written a helpful article about how lying stems from childhood protective defenses ("Sexual Addiction and the Amazing Lie-O-Matic," http://sexual-addict.com/sexual_addiction_and_the _amazing).

50. See chapters 13, 14, and 17 of my book *When to Walk Away*.

51. See Joe Dallas, *The Game Plan: The Men's 30-Day Strategy for Attaining Sexual Integrity* (Nashville: Nelson, 2005), 33–34.

52. St. Ambrose, "On the Decease of His Brother Satyrus," Book I, 1–4,

EWTN, www.ewtn.com/catholicism/teachings/st-ambrose-on-the-death
-of-his-brother-193.

53. Cited in Cara Plett, "Mourning in Marriage after the Loss of a Child,"
Focus on the Family Canada, www.focusonthefamily.ca/content
/mourning-in-marriage-after-the-loss-of-a-child.

54. Parrotts, *I Love You More*, 142.

55. Parrotts, *I Love You More*, 144, italics in original.

56. Parrotts, *I Love You More*, 152.

57. Parrotts, *I Love You More*, 153.

58. Parrotts, *I Love You More*, 153.

59. Parrotts, *I Love You More*, 154.

CONNECTING WITH GARY

While Gary isn't available to answer personal emails, he's happy to hear from you. You can connect with him via his website: www.garythomas.com.

TWITTER: @GaryLThomas

FACEBOOK: AuthorGaryThomas

INSTAGRAM: GaryThomasBooks

BLOG: www.garythomasbooks.substack.com

Married Sex

A Christian Couple's Guide to Reimagining Your Love Life

Gary Thomas and Debra Fileta, M.A., LPC

A great sex life is something you make, not something you find. If you feel confused or frustrated about your sex life—or simply wonder, *Is there more to it than this?—Married Sex* is exactly what you need to make your marriage stronger, both in and out of the bedroom.

Including the stories of real-life couples, research results from hundreds of comprehensive surveys, and professional perspective from a bestselling spiritual writer and a licensed counselor, *Married Sex* will:

- Help you understand why married sex is one of God's best ideas
- Teach you the inner workings of your body and your spouse's body in order to achieve optimal pleasure
- Guide you through the most common sexual problems couples have and what to do about them
- Help you see how your past experiences and expectations influence your present sex life
- Give you practical suggestions and techniques to enhance your sexual experience
- Encourage you to take ownership in the process of making love, seeing a great sex life as a beautiful opportunity to honor both God and your spouse

Psychology, theology, research, story, and let's-get-started ideas combine to make *Married Sex* a resource for you and your spouse like no other book you've read before. Discover practical, biblically informed answers to your questions about intimacy as you find more satisfaction in your marriage than ever.

Available in stores and online!

ZONDERVAN®
.com